UNMASKING
THE JEZEBEL SPIRIT

JOHN PAUL JACKSON

KINGSWAY PUBLICATIONS
EASTBOURNE

Copyright © John Paul Jackson 2001

First published in the USA by Streams Publications
First British edition 2001
Reprinted 2002 (twice), 2003

All rights reserved.
No part of this book may be reproduced or
transmitted in any form or by any means, electronic
or mechanical, including photocopy, recording, or any
information storage and retrieval systems, without
permission in writing from the publisher.

Unless otherwise indicated, all Scripture quotations are from
The New King James Version copyright © 1979, 1980, 1982
by Thomas Nelson, Inc.

ISBN 0 85476 993 5

Published by
KINGSWAY COMMUNICATIONS
Lottbridge Drove, Eastbourne BN23 6NT, England.
Email: books@kingsway.co.uk

Book design and production for the publishers by
Bookprint Creative Services, P.O. Box 827, BN21 3YJ, England.
Printed in Great Britain.

Reproduced from the original text by arrangement with
Streams Publications

CONTENTS

*To the hundreds of pastors
who have shared their stories,
to the many prophetic voices who have
been silenced at the hands of this spirit,
to the intercessors who have been
crushed under the weight of this
oppressive foe; may you find
healing from the pain.*

*To those who have
succumbed to this spirit
and recovered, may your gifts
one day be used to
further the glorious
Kingdom of God.*

ACKNOWLEDGEMENTS

MANY PEOPLE ARE INVOLVED in the making of a book. First, my dearest expression of appreciation goes to my beloved wife, Diane. She has continually encouraged me and offered valuable insights throughout the fifteen years it has taken to write this book. Many demonic attacks have caused me to shelve this book several times. Yet the Lord kept speaking and saying, "Don't give up on it."

Diane has valiantly weathered each harrassing storm the enemy sent our way to abort this book's publication. Her prayers, insights, and keen ability to hear the voice of the Lord have enriched this manuscript, as well as my own life. This book may prove to be the most difficult book that I will ever have to write.

I want to acknowledge the efforts of all who contributed to this book. My heartfelt thanks goes to Marla Wessel who assisted me fifteen years ago in developing the original manuscript. I wish to thank three intercessors who made valuable suggestions to the manuscript: Tina Santizo, Linda Nail, and Jo Beth Kested. I also wish to thank those who lovingly proofread the manuscript: Randa Rottschafer, Jane Mitrani, Diane Schechner, Laura Smith, Fenancia Tillema, Ruth Armstrong, Laurie Thompson, Kyndl Sanchez, Vicki Jackson, and Roxanne Stewart.

I want to acknowledge Carolyn Blunk, who served as the managing editor on this project, and her assistant editor, Brett Yates. Their hours of hard work and dedication have turned my meager attempt into a helpful treatise for the Kingdom of God. I also want to thank Hank Sword whose beautiful designs frame this book.

My heartfelt appreciation goes to Lou Engle who wrote the foreword and to my dear friends who sent their endorsements to encourage others to read and capture the glorious destiny of a coming prophetic generation.

Finally, I want to express my appreciation to my staff at Streams Ministries International for helping me carry the spiritual weight of this exposé. They, in turn, have had to face their own battles as Satan has sought to stop this book from being printed.

Through God we will do valiantly, for it is
He who shall tread down our enemies–Psalm 60:12.

INTRODUCTION

I N THIS BOOK, I have recounted the stories of many who have battled the Jezebel spirit. I hope the lessons and experiences chronicled in this book will be an encouragement to you. However, in reading this book please do not make the mistake of assuming that women are the only ones influenced by this demonic spirit. While it is true that the only clear examples in Scripture were women, I believe that men such as Absalom, Korah, and Balaam operated under this spirit.

I pray that pastors, in reading this book, will restrain themselves from casting stones at the innocent or anyone who disagrees with them. I also pray that they will not mistakenly perceive those with a growing prophetic gift, who are simply immature in church protocol, as having a Jezebel spirit. Hence, throughout the book I have tried to point out the differences between these two spirits, along with some suggested remedies.

Finally, in reading this book, I trust that you will not come to the conclusion that I am against strong, anointed women in ministry. Nothing could be further from the truth! In fact, I was prompted to accept God's call on my life by a very powerful and anointed woman, the late Ruth Ward Heflin.

In 1981, Ruth had been given a dream while living in Jerusalem. The Lord told Ruth to go to Dallas, Texas. She would be given time on a radio show to discuss how God speaks through dreams and visions. The Lord told her that a young man would be listening to the broadcast who was resisting the call of God on his life. He had given this young man dreams and visions. During the talk show, the young man would call in. She would be used to change the direction of his life and help him fulfill his destiny. I was that young man.

So, please understand that I highly value women fulfilling their call in Christ. In the last days, many godly women will arise with an anointing to predict and demonstrate awesome signs and wonders. While many women will exert a boldness, fierceness, and determination that to some might appear overpowering, their lives will also exude submission to God's appointed authority, as all our lives must.

We are on the threshold of the greatest move of God in the history of the world. God wants to visit us in an unprecedented way. This book was written as a call to a prophetic generation that was foretold in Scripture by the prophet Joel. He described a remarkable generation that would have the spirit of God poured out upon them without measure (Joel 2:28-32). Under the anointing of the Holy Spirit, prophetic utterances would arise from both men and women, young and old.

Historically, wherever prophetic voices are being raised up, the enemy will raise up counterfeit voices that mimic the prophetic anointing. That voice is the Jezebel spirit. In this book, I will focus on how Jezebel, as a celestial power, influences the actions of individuals. Knowingly or unknowingly, these individuals will hinder and oppose the move of God in this age.

It is my prayer that God's divine order will come into prominence and that the Church will be aroused from its complacency and tolerance of this spirit. I also pray that God-breathed prophetic ministry and godly intercessors, bearing the mark of humility, wisdom, and discernment, will arise and help to usher in the glorious Kingdom of our Lord.

To learn more about John Paul Jackson and his courses,
contact:

Streams Ministries International
PO Box 550
Sutton
New Hampshire 03260
USA

Email: info@streamsministries.com
Website: www.streamsministries.com

Chapter 1

AN AGE OF APOSTASY

IT WAS AN AGE of apostasy. A nation whom God had called to be His own turned against Him. They exchanged their worship of God for the idols of a people they had once conquered in His name. The king who ruled Israel was the son of a man who gained his kingship through assassination. His name, Ahab, was to become a synonym for evil.

Behind the corruption of Ahab's throne was a woman—Jezebel. Hoping to expand her power by marrying Ahab, she brought destruction on the Israelites. This destruction came through her fanatical devotion to the false gods—Baal, the male deity of power and sexuality, and Ashtoreth, the female goddess of fertility, love, and war. Baal and Ashtoreth rituals involved depraved and licentious sexual practices and abominations. The worship of these idols appealed to the bestial and material elements in human nature. The Baal idol resembled the male sexual organ while the altar to Ashtaroth resembled the female sexual organ. More than 450 prophets of Baal and 400 prophetesses of Ashtoreth served Jezebel's depraved and carnal desires. Human lives were often sacrificed to appease her pagan deities.

Against this apostasy, God raised up the prophet Elijah who challenged Ahab and destroyed the prophets of Baal on Mt. Carmel. As a countermove, Satan raised up his messenger to silence God's prophetic voice. It came through Ahab's wife—Queen Jezebel.

We, too, are living in an age of apostasy. Our society has turned its back on God. Sin has infected the Body of Christ and its leaders. Yet, in the midst of the incredible decadence and depravity of our day, God is raising up a prophetic generation. This generation will carry the spirit of Elijah. They will be anointed to perform miraculous signs and wonders and accomplish great exploits for the Kingdom of God.

Just as he has done from the beginning, Satan is raising up a fierce opposition to this prophetic generation. The enemy has always sought to silence God's prophetic voices and abort intercessory prayer. Again, its name is Jezebel—a diabolical spiritual force that seeks to deceive, defile, and destroy God's authorities.

While the term "Jezebel spirit" is used in some charismatic circles, few people truly understand how this demonic force operates. A Jezebel spirit is a celestial power that has worldwide influence. It is not simply a demon that possesses an individual. It is a demonic power in the heavenly realm that transcends specific geographical boundaries and can affect nations. Whatever region this power enters, it co-joins and collaborates with the ruling principality of that territory.

Jezebelic powers operate in conjunction with principalities and powers that torment people (Ephesians 6:12). These demonic powers include spirits of religion, manipulation, control, lust, perversion, and the occult. These spirits often work in concert with a Jezebel spirit to build strongholds in a person's mind.

When a Jezebelic stronghold is established in a person's mind, I define this as "coming under the influence of a Jezebel spirit." At the moment this occurs, the individual's rational, reasoning process begins to deteriorate. His or her thoughts and actions become distorted.

For those familiar with computers, you might say that the computer of their mind has received a virus that causes it to respond to data in a non-logical manner. It corrupts, re-routes and distorts all information received from that point forward. Like a computer virus, a Jezebelic stronghold is programmed to manifest when certain keystrokes—or situations—arise. The virus also influences the activity of others in their network. In fact, a Jezebel spirit, like a virus, is designed to shut down the network and kill the host. This also occurs with anyone who does not disconnect from the host.

An anti-virus program will alert the computer to the fact that a virus is operating contrary to the laws of the computer program for which it was designed. The anti-virus program then tells the computer how to recognize the virus and discard it. To operate effectively, a computer may need to be reprogrammed with new data—depending on the degree of damage caused by the virus.

This illustration dramatically parallels what happens in the Kingdom when an alien force—a Jezebel power—is downloaded into a church. Its goal is to disable and destroy individuals, ministries, and the church. This will be the result unless God's remedy—a divine antivirus—is applied. If pastors are unable to prevent or detect this spirit's operation, their spouses, children, and church members may fall prey to this overwhelming spirit.

From time to time, all of us are vulnerable to being influenced by this controlling and manipulative power. We all try to contol others to some extent. And while there are no clear-cut indicators of when a person steps over the line, opening your soul to operating in a Jezebel spirit is a process that occurs over time. The longer someone operates in a controlling and manipulative way without repenting from doing so, the stronger this spirit grows. Eventually, it will become a way of life for those with this spirit. The primary method for relating to others and gaining control will be through this spirit.

Although the illustrations in Scripture of Jezebel are female-oriented, this demonic power does not simply infect women. Men have operated in this spirit as well. When this occurs they are left weakened and emasculated by the demonic presence. However, it is difficult for men to operate under the influence of this spirit for very long because it needs an Ahab spirit to keep it alive. Instead, the Jezebel spirit commonly operates through women, who use the allure and seduction of this spirit to accomplish their objectives.

By writing this book, I seek to facilitate healing and unity in the Body of Christ. Therefore, I want to caution anyone when applying the term, "Jezebel spirit." As

Christians, we do not want to hurt people unnecessarily—maligning and falsely accusing them. In fact, we can actually take on the characteristics of Jezebel—a murderous spirit—when we hunt people down and falsely label them.

We must keep in mind that most of those influenced by this spirit are hurting and wounded individuals. The power of the Holy Spirit is available to help heal those who are afflicted by this spirit.

Jesus longs to set us free from what ensnares us. We must all look at our sin, and that of others, with honesty, compassion and hope. Ministry to people and churches oppressed by this spirit is desperately needed today. Now is the time for courageous grace by pastors and leaders.

Chapter 2
UNHOLY ALLIANCES

NELSON TOOK ANOTHER sip of coffee and continued to watch the attractive young woman. She was tastefully dressed in a dark suit and had the look of optimism—a confident handshake and direct eye contact, while soulfully engaging people in conversation. With her penetrating charisma, the woman was vivacious and enthusiastic. She had the ability to draw people to her. She was fun to be with and seemed to be a devoted student of the Bible.

As Nelson's church was beginning to shrink, individuals that he had earmarked for leadership had left. To fill their void, he needed to find new leaders. Each month his desperation increased, as the money from tithes and offerings continued to shrink. During their times together, the woman suggested her theories on how to increase church membership. An extremely savvy businesswoman, she created a blueprint to steer the church towards a position of dominance. Over the ensuing months, she became more entrenched in the church and began to lead a women's Bible study group.

At the same time, Nelson was puzzled by the woman's beliefs. She seemed to be in touch with the Spirit. However, it seemed to be a "dark spirit" that told her to do some unusual things, some of which had previously resulted in immorality. Despite this, Nelson and his wife, loved being around her. Seeing her potential, they met with the woman often and even attempted to mentor her.

As they placed their hopes in her, young women in the church began to rally around this woman. While her influence grew, Nelson's seemed to diminish. Like a slow leaking tire, the church was beginning to shrink. Then, Nelson's wife began to suffer various illnesses and his mind became filled with sexual fantasies. To make matters worse, his once amiable church staff became divisive and their vibrant small-groups program began to dwindle.

One day, Nelson called and asked me for help. As I began to seek God, a dream came allowing me to see through the enemy's smoke screen. I relayed what God had shown me, which was affirmed as accurate. Yet Nelson and his wife seemed torn. Stalled by indecision and confusion, they continued to give the woman responsibility, leadership, and authority within the church. They admitted that she might occasionally receive counsel from a "spirit guide." Nonetheless, they loved this woman and wanted to help her. What were they to do?

AN UNHOLY ALLIANCE

What I have just described is called an unholy alliance—a relationship that allows you to meet your end results, even though you are aware that the person willfully continues to sin. Furthermore, it is evident from Scripture that God does not sanction such a person being given a leadership position within the church. Although Nelson and his wife justified their decision to not remove this woman from leadership "for the sake of the Kingdom," the Kingdom was compromised by the unholy arrangement, and ultimately, their church suffered.

DIVIDED LOYALTIES

A similar situation happened with Omri, Israel's sixth king. To secure and enlarge his kingdom Omri forged an unholy alliance through the marriage of his son, Ahab, to a foreign bride, Jezebel. This created a political bond between Israel and Tyre. The marriage was meant to seal a peace treaty between the two powers; however, the alliance proved to be a costly compromise. Ceremonially, it required that Israel follow the religious and political protocols of Ahab's new wife. This meant furthering the immersion of Israel into idolatry. Therefore, by his plan to enlarge his kingdom, Omri actually positioned the Israelites in harm's way. His need to build a glorious nation blinded him to the consequences of lawlessness.

By agreeing to take a foreign queen, Ahab knowingly violated God's command. Apparently, he justified his actions in his own mind, but the Lord condemned Ahab as having sold himself to wickedness (1 Kings 21:25). As a zealous participant in the depraved worship of Baal, a political alliance would have officially endorsed Jezebel's immoral and idolatrous religious beliefs and inflicted them upon the Israelites. History tells us that is precisely what happened.

Jezebel brought her vile religious practices to Israel. She mandated that stone idols be set atop the high places and also erected in God's holy temple. Even if she did nothing else, this flagrant decree alone caused her to be hated by the prophets of Israel. Thus, Jezebel exchanged the holy for the profane. Scripture also indicates that Jezebel was a harlot and an adulteress as well as a practitioner of witchcraft (2 Kings 9:22).

Jezebel had personality characteristics that revolved around manipulation, control, sexual perversion, and idolatry. Some rather startling and relevant conclusions can be made about a woman who strikes such a tone of vengeance in the heart of the Lord. I believe an evil spirit motivated Jezebel's actions and bestowed upon her widespread influence. I also believe the influence of this spirit exists today and has never been eradicated from the Church. Instead, it has enjoyed an unholy reign. As we near the last days, this demonic spirit seems even more entrenched in the Church.

The name, Jezebel, is Phoenician in origin and means "un-husbanded." Although she was married, Jezebel's lack of submission and her infidelities proved marriage meant nothing to her. While marriage is a picture of mutual respect and submission, Jezebel submitted to no one. Instead, she required that everyone submit to her. Her marriage was merely a political alliance that enabled her to become not simply the queen, but in essence, the acting king! She held the answers to all of the king's problems.

DEADLY DIVA

Jezebel learned treachery from her father, Ethbaal, whose name meant "like unto Baal." Ethbaal had become king by plotting murder. Thereby, Jezebel's penchant for murder had generational roots. Eliminating someone's life was merely incidental to achieving an objective.

We are first introduced to Jezebel during the reign of Ahab, king of Israel, 869-850 BC (1 Kings 16:31). Ahab was not the only one to succumb to Jezebel's perversions. Jezebel's children yielded to their mother's control. Her son, Ahaziah, was guilty of the sins of his father (1 Kings 22:51-53). Another son, Joram, was killed by Jehu, King of Israel, as punishment for all the things his parents had done to God's prophets (2 Kings 9:24-26).

Jezebel's daughter, Athaliah, became queen of Judah. Just like her mother, she looked for a husband who was weak so that she could carry out her evil practices (2 Kings 8:25-27). As a result, her own son, Ahaziah, who was named after her brother and may have been conceived through their incestuous relationship, did evil in the sight of the Lord. Both mother and son, as well as the seventy other sons of Ahab and their families, suffered death at the order of Jehu.

Jezebel was no ordinary woman. She had a flair for the dramatic. Every action she took, every word she spoke must have been done with great passion and unholy abandonment. She was an intimidating figure, a rose with razor sharp thorns. She was impossible to ignore, because to do so could cost you your life.

The way Jezebel greeted Jehu at the top of the wall was more than a casual hello. She painted her eyes and picked out the most alluring gown she could find. She planned a seductive maneuver to entice Jehu, Israel's tenth king (2 Kings 9:6), and to lure him into forming an alliance with her—perhaps to become her next husband. If nothing else, she sought to intimidate Jehu. She was a dominant force in Israel. If Jehu had not ordered her thrown from the wall, Jezebel would have had the kingdom to herself. However, Jehu bravely carried out the task the Lord had given him—to do away with the house of Ahab (2 Kings 9:7).

In this hour, God is issuing a call to pastors around the world. Will they respond as Ahab or Jehu?

Peace At Any Cost

A spirit of Ahab symbolizes the abdication of authority, or at the very least, passive authority. It bespeaks of a mind-set that avoids confrontation and denies fault. The spirit of Ahab loves the position it has and fears confrontation. Someone with an Ahab spirit would rather make peace at any cost, even if it leads to making unholy alliances.

An individual under the influence of an Ahab spirit will often make truces instead of covenants, thus prostituting rather than sanctifying the relationship. How can you have a truce with someone whose goal is to destroy you? An Ahab spirit will always sacrifice the future for the sake of peace today.

Working in tandem, the spirits of Ahab and Jezebel quietly form a codependent relationship. Both will need and feed off the other in order to accomplish their goals, much like a parasite and its host. A pastor influenced by an Ahab spirit will need the help of someone with a Jezebel spirit, in order to maintain position and to entrench their powerbase.

A pastor friend, Russell, kept searching for a specific woman in his church for me to meet. While this is not unusual—nor is it wrong in itself—Russell appeared to be relying too heavily on this woman's input into every decision he made. I cautioned him about codependent relationships, but it was too late. Six months later, Russell fell into sexual sin with this woman.

PLACATING LEADERS

Like many leaders today, Ahab's reign was characterized by trying to placate and pacify Jezebel's demands. He tolerated Jezebel's abominable decrees and practices.

Many pastors embrace an individual influenced by a Jezebel spirit because the person appears to have leadership skills or spiritual insight that will help a church grow. Some may even convince themselves that, in time, they will spiritually "mature" the individual. But in the process of helping this individual, many pastors strike a compromise and weaken their authority. Remember, Ahab's placating spirit is exactly what gave rise to Jezebel's lethal powerbase.

On several occasions, I have watched pastors remain indecisive and non-confrontational simply out of fear that an individual would split their church. One particular pastor was very aware that his chief intercessor operated with a Jezebel spirit. He was afraid to address the situation simply because she was intimidating and had influence over others. If he lost any more church members, he would default on his church loan payment. Unfortunately, this situation characterizes many pastors today. Prayer and encouragement are needed for pastors who are caught in this deadly snare.

AVOIDING CONFRONTATIONS

It takes a courageous pastor to confront the strength and obstinacy of a Jezebel spirit. By their actions, an individual with a Jezebel spirit will reveal a pastor's strengths and weaknesses. Pastors will see things about themselves that they might rather ignore. He or she may react defensively when their authority is challenged. To quell a revolt, the pastor may respond by appeasing or promoting this spirit. Becoming fearful, he or she may decide to suppress all prophetic gifts in their church. Or the pastor may selfishly even use this person to promote their own agenda. Any of these responses will damage the spiritual life of a church. Left unchecked, the pastor will leave his or her church open to domination and control by this diabolical spirit. The church will quickly sink beneath the increasing weight of spiritual oppression, crushing healthy spiritual vitality and vision.

A Jezebel spirit will defile everything it touches. That which is holy will become vile. People will begin to leave a church, not knowing why; they simply feel compelled to go, as if they could feel the impending darkness.

Pastors who overreact and impulsively eliminate intercessory and prophetic groups will silence their most reliable sources of discernment and revelation. When this happens, a spiritual vacuum will be created in their church. The darkness of confusion will quickly rush in. As in a game of chess, if you leave a space unoccupied, your opponent may soon seize that ground. Such a maneuver may allow the enemy to position his own deadly prophets in key places.

Pastors who retreat from exercising their authority may bring injury upon God's people by inadvertently allowing the increased rule of this demonic spirit. As long as the issue is avoided, the problem will only worsen. When it is finally challenged, a Jezebel spirit that has become entrenched in a church is more difficult to dislodge.

CONSPIRING WITH DARKNESS

If a pastor feigns ignorance of Jezebel's wrongdoing, he or she may become a kindred spirit. Knowingly or unknowingly, the pastor has aligned himself or herself with this spirit. Their methods and goals will begin to parallel one another. A pastor will also quickly discover that he or she can accomplish their goals by exploiting their spiritual mirror image, becoming a conspirator with darkness.

One of two judgments will come to this pastor, unless he or she sees their error and repents. They will either fully embrace a Jezebel spirit and become a puppet king subject to strong delusion, heavy depression, and indecision even in the smallest matters. Or, they and their church will face a spiritual famine. God's manifest presence will be removed from their midst. Only the memory of His presence will remain; sadly they will not perceive this as God's judgment.

TOLERATING THE ENEMY

Nevertheless I have a few things against you,
because you allow that woman Jezebel, who
calls herself a prophetess, to teach and seduce
My servants to commit sexual immorality and
eat things sacrificed to idols—Revelation 2:20.

When a pastor has a trusted friend who begins to show traits of the Jezebel spirit, it becomes easy for the pastor to justify the person's rebellion or to simply ignore it.

Generally, pastors demonstrate tolerance toward those they call, "friends." However, your trust and loyalty to a friend will create a blind spot. A pastor, therefore, will need to step outside the friendship, view the situation as a pastoral issue and correct any rebellion.

Ultimately, if a pastor brings correction, people will feel secure under a pastor's leadership and develop trust in godly authority. However, if a pastor fails to correct rebellion, he or she will eventually lose the people's respect. Church members will regard the pastor with disdain because of the consequences brought upon their church. Confusion will arise and God's purposes will become obscured by a waffling leadership.

A pastor who compromises will attract people who compromise. The pastor's anointing will be reduced to a mere drop compared to what it was meant to be. The light from their churches will grow dim as the Body begins to lose its spiritual cutting edge.

FRUITS OF TOLERANCE

But there was no one like Ahab who sold himself to do wickedness in the sight of the Lord, because Jezebel his wife stirred him up—
1 Kings 21:25.

Just as Ahab permitted Jezebel to sacrifice children as a form of worship, the driving spirit behind abortion in the United States is kept alive by the Jezebel spirit. Through self-promoting, controlling, and manipulative schemes, this spirit also seeks to abort those who are young or immature in the Lord. Moreover, this spirit welcomes false teachers who are driven by the intellectual power of the soul.

The hour has come for a new mandate. It is rising up the land and gaining momentum. God is empowering His Church with boldness and zeal brought about by true apostolic and prophetic voices. In this hour, God desires the spirit of prophecy, which is the testimony of Jesus, to be vibrant in every church. The prophetic spirit will reveal that which is hidden.

VICTORIOUS BATTLES

Thus says the Lord God of Israel: 'I have anointed you king over the people of the Lord, over Israel...that I may avenge the blood of My servants the prophets, and the blood of all the servants of the Lord, at the hand of Jezebel—2 Kings 9:6-7.

At this point in history, a great battle awaits God's representatives—the shepherds of His Church. Pastors are being summoned by the Lord to take on the spirit of valor and to stand up as true kings. Just as Jehu's commission was to rid God's Kingdom of the defiling and demoralizing influences of Ahab and Jezebel, a call is going forth today to remove those same apostate spirits from the Church.

Chapter 3

A CORRUPTING INFLUENCE

I N AN EPISODE OF Star Trek: Deep Space Nine entitled, "Paradise Lost," aliens known as changelings infiltrated key positions in Starfleet. These aliens had assumed human form and taken the appearance of trusted members of the Federation. Their purpose was to create confusion and fear on the Earth. Just as the changelings sent their agents to sabotage the Federation, Satan sends his own dark forces to disrupt the work of the Church. These demonic agents may assume our appearance and speak our language, but their allegiance is to another kingdom. Just as the Federation needed to learn to discern the presence of changelings, so the Body of Christ needs to identify those operating under a spirit of Jezebel.

Scott, who pastored a very large Midwestern church, was puzzled about the multiple defections in his leadership. He had carefully chosen and trained a remarkable team. He now suspected that another staff member was leaving. Then, the light began to dawn. One of his staff members met with a woman who had once been a member of a witch's coven. She incidentally mentioned that she recognized two women who regularly attended the church as being witches from her former coven. Although it was assumed they were Christians, it was later discovered they were still practicing witchcraft. During the church services, the duo would sit on the front row and quietly chant under their breath. Tragically, these witches were able to derail Scott's strong leadership team by sending demonic curses against them.

TAKE WARNING

The apostle John gave a warning to the Church at Thyatira, a city in Asia Minor, concerning a person who had embraced the Jezebel spirit.

> Nevertheless I have a few things against you, because you allow that woman Jezebel, who calls herself a prophetess, to teach and seduce My servants to commit sexual immorality and eat things sacrificed to idols. And I gave her time to repent of her sexual immorality, and she did not repent. Indeed I will cast her into a sickbed, and those who commit adultery with her into great tribulation, unless they repent of their deeds. I will kill her children with death, and all the churches shall know that I am He who searches the minds and hearts. And I will give to each one of you

according to your works. Now to you I say, and to the rest in Thyatira, as many as do not have this doctrine, who have not known the depths of Satan, as they say, I will put on you no other burden. But hold fast what you have till I come. And he who overcomes, and keeps My works until the end, to him I will give power over the nations—He shall rule them with a rod of iron; they shall be dashed to pieces like the potter's vessels—as I also have received from My Father; and I will give him the morning star—Revelation 2:20-28.

Imagine how the Church in Thyatira felt when they read "I have this against you...." (Revelation 2:4). God gave them a choice: remove the unrepentant Jezebel or suffer God's judgment. Few, if any, decrees are as dreadful as this one. To fall under God's judgment is a fearful thing. When God resists you, nothing you do will prosper. As you come out from under His protection, you will be powerless before principalities and powers.

Removing an unrepentant person from a church is the same principle by which the produce manager at a grocery store does "freshness checks" throughout the day. He knows that one peach with a rotten spot can spoil the entire barrel because the decaying acid will spread to other peaches. Eventually, the whole barrel will go bad because of one bad peach. Therefore, rotten produce has to be identified and removed in order to save the remaining peaches.

This principle of removing sin from the whole Body was why the apostle Paul commanded the Church in Corinth to remove the young man who was sexually immoral with his father's wife. One man's sin will infect an entire church much like a little leaven or yeast spreads throughout bread dough (1 Corinthians 5:1-12). This was the situation facing the Church at Thyatira. Jezebel's influence was corrupting the church and defiling many. She and her influence had to be identified and removed in order to prevent an entire church from being defiled and disgraced.

LEADING BONDSERVANTS ASTRAY

Jesus warned the Church at Thyatira about this spirit. Jezebel seeks to destroy and silence God's prophets because in doing so, she destroys the testimony of Jesus, which *is* the spirit of prophecy (Revelation 19:10). By calling herself a "prophetess," Jezebel was teaching and leading God's bondservants astray.

Over the centuries, many of the Lord's bondservants, apostles, and prophets have been attacked by the Jezebel spirit. Those who survive the campaign of this spirit will often vacate their church posts and move to other locations. Until a pastor finally uses his or her godly authority to remove this spirit from their congregation, mature prophetic voices will stay away. Meanwhile, the Jezebel spirit will seek to implant its own demonic prophets in a church in order to teach the deep things of Satan.

Whenever a pastor fears an individual or a demonic spirit more than God, in essence, the pastor is unwittingly admitting, "This spirit is more powerful than God." More than likely this was how the Church at Thyatira came to accept the woman Jezebel as a prophetess and a teacher. Obviously they knew her problems, because Scripture says they tolerated her and knowingly indulged her deviant beliefs and practices. More than likely, they were intimidated by her ruthless control and insubordination. Subsequently, she procured a church leadership position.

To agree with a Jezebel spirit is portrayed in Scripture as committing spiritual fornication with her. By allowing Jezebel to remain in leadership, God was forced to bring judgment not *only* upon Jezebel but upon the church as well (Revelation 2:22). This, however, could have been avoided simply by removing the unrepentant individual.

GOD'S JUDGMENTS

...and all the churches shall know that I am
He who searches the minds and hearts—
Revelation 2:23.

What a solemn and challenging responsibility faced the pastor in Thyatira! Not only was the Lord going to let all the churches know the results of what happened, but He was going to let them know the judgment—or the blessing—that would happen in Thyatira. In doing so, God not only judged their actions but the motives hidden deep within the recesses of their hearts that allowed them to tolerate her lawlessness.

A SINGULAR BURDEN

...I will put on you no other burden—
Revelation 2:24.

This simple, yet overlooked phrase indicates the singular weight of importance that God gave to removing this spirit. The Church at Thyatira was charged with only one task—to remove Jezebel. Since God referred to the task as a "burden," we can sense the extreme difficulty of removing a prophetess who was in leadership. Undoubtedly, it would involve a devoted effort by all the other church leaders, as well as the entire church body, to overcome this morally compromising influence.

I believe that God chose Thyatira to be an example to us today. From that time on, churches around the world would look to this church to learn how and why they must handle this diabolical spirit.

Overcoming a Jezebel spirit will require more than simply ending the self-proclaimed and self-anointed rule of individuals who advertise their spiritual gifts. It also requires that God's leaders humble themselves and repent from using their God-given authority in an unrighteous way.

A PASTOR WHO CRIED "JEZEBEL"

Michael seemed very self-assured and confident. Yet, beneath his charming exterior, he was full of insecurities. At this his second pastorate, Michael faced complaints from church members that reminded him of his first pastorate. Anticipating another failed situation, he began to respond defensively and harshly to any criticism. He grew suspicious and controlling. Easily provoked, Michael would shift the blame for various problems onto others—often charging innocent people with "having a Jezebel spirit."

Three years later, a new couple began attending his church. Yet after several surprising encounters, Michael realized that both the husband and wife operated under a mature Jezebel spirit. There was only one problem: Michael had used the term "Jezebel" so many times that no one believed him now.

To make matters worse, the leadership began to point a finger at Michael's own issues of control and manipulation. Thrown off balance by their suspicions, Michael felt as if he was the person on trial. Six months later, this couple boldly proclaimed in a Sunday morning service they were "anointed by God" to pastor the church. A week later, Michael was forced to resign and the couple became co-pastors. Within a year, however, the church closed its doors.

UNRIGHTEOUS AUTHORITY

...for in whatever you judge another you condemn yourself; for you who judge practice the same thing—Romans 2:1.

Michael, in pointing the finger, was condemning himself. His actions only served to empower the Jezebel spirit in his church. If he had not been guilty of the same issues, Michael would have recognized the difference between the innocent and the immature. He would have also avoided the painful consequences that ensued.

Pastors and leaders must recognize, and then relinquish, *any* methods of control and manipulation they exercise. They must cease to gossip against fellow pastors and other believers. (A hint that you may be having problems in this area would be if you find yourself talking disrespectfully about other ministries or if you reveal personal tidbits shared in confidence with you.) Pastors, who have privileged information, are sometimes the worst offenders. They must refrain from gossip, before the wineskin tears.

Making private accusations and listening to accusations without a proper witness also needs to cease. Pastors must avoid capitalizing upon and exploiting their church members' spirituality, coercing them to do what the pastor wants done. This is called "domination." It is a fleshly counterfeit of what it means to righteously exercise spiritual influence and authority. To overcome a Jezebel spirit requires that leaders address all rebellion and usurped authority committed by one church member against another. To do this, they must be free of these issues as well.

In order for the flock to understand proper authority, leaders need to teach on biblical authority. Overcoming a Jezebel spirit involves recognizing and restoring any relationship that was overturned and any God-ordained authority that was stolen by this spirit. I will address this more fully in later chapters.

THE REWARDS OF RIGHTEOUS AUTHORITY

...And I will give to each one of you according to your works—Revelation 2:23b.

Exercising righteous authority has a reward that corresponds to the very thing we have overcome. The pastor who overcomes a Jezebel spirit that seeks to usurp his or her rule will be given a greater sphere of rule and authority. This was what the apostle John said when he wrote the Lord's admonition to the Church in Thyatira:

And he who overcomes, and keeps My works until the end, to him I will give power over the nations—He shall rule them with a rod of iron; they shall be dashed to pieces like the potter's vessels—as I also have received from

My Father; and I will give him the morning
star—Revelation 2:26-28.

Three promises are given to those who overcome a
Jezebel spirit. First, they will be given widespread spiritual
authority over principalities, powers, and spiritual rulers in
high places, now as well as in the age to come. By breaking
this spirit's power on Earth—individual by individual—it
disintegrates the rule of those powers in the heavenlies.

Second, pastors will be given authority to rule "with a
rod of iron." The only other place "a rod of iron" is mentioned
is in Revelation 19:15 when it speaks of Jesus. Ruling with
a rod of iron does not mean being tyrannical. Rather, one
who so rules will find his or her authority conditioned by
great wisdom. By assuming the role of Jehu concerning any
dark spirit, leaders will uphold the discipline and principles
of the Word of God. When a pastor is like a rod of iron, he or
she cannot be easily bent or manipulated. This will be the
level of power and authority given by God to those who overcome a Jezebel spirit.

Third, the Lord will grant the "morning star" to the
overcomer of the Jezebel spirit (Revelation 2:26-28; 2 Peter
1:19). The morning star referred to in this passage is divine
authority and favor.

Both rewards—the rod of iron and the morning
star—differ from other rewards recorded in Revelation and
they are unique to this church. Moreover, they carry much
greater authority than is evidenced today. Although none of
the other churches mentioned in Revelation received these
three particular promises, neither did they face the formidable task of confronting and removing a Jezebel spirit.

WATCHMEN AT THE GATE

It is imperative to be discerning about those who bring destruction to the Church. It is, therefore, the role of humble intercessors to stand as watchmen at the Church's gate. It is an intercessor's responsibility to sound the alarm when they discern someone who might injure the fold. Consequently, it is vital for every church to have a strong intercessory ministry in order to prevent the spirit of Jezebel from doing its destructive work.

How does a pastor discern who are the true watchmen? On the television episode of Star Trek: Deep Space Nine, the changelings were quickly discerned by a simple blood test. Although they looked human, they were bloodless. Likewise, true watchmen can be discerned by what is inside of them. There are several ways their true spirit becomes evident. One way is through their words. Jesus said:

> ...For out of the abundance of the heart the mouth speaks. A good man out of the good treasure of his heart brings forth good things, and an evil man out of the evil treasure brings forth evil things—Matthew 12:34-35.

If Jezebelic tendencies exist in an intercessor's heart, then eventually it will be revealed through their speech and/or actions. Often they will sow lawlessness or divisiveness in a church. However, a true watchman does not use his or her position to challenge and belittle pastoral authority. Rather, the intercessor humbly lifts them up by praying for them. Furthermore, a true watchman does *not* seek authority, but he or she prays for those who have authority.

Another way a true watchman becomes evident is by the fruit of his or her spirit. Scripture clearly defines what the fruits of the Spirit are:

> But the fruit of the Spirit is love, joy, peace, longsuffering, kindness, goodness, faithfulness, gentleness, self-control. Against such there is no law—Galatians 5:22-23.

We must watch to see and to know those who labor among us. We must not simply know them on the surface, but we must know them deeply—what they believe, what they listen to and what they say when they pray.

> Either make the tree good and its fruit good, or else make the tree bad and its fruit bad; for a tree is known by its fruit—Matthew 12:33.

A true watchman is submissive to authority, whereas someone operating under a Jezebel spirit usurps authority. In a best-case scenario, a watchman who is submitted to the Holy Spirit has the same attitude as David when he served Saul—one of restraint and respect to God's chosen authority:

> The Lord forbid that I should stretch out my hand against the Lord's anointed—1 Samuel 26:11a.

Finally, the most obvious difference between a true watchman and an individual operating with a Jezebel spirit is the motivation, or driving force, behind his or her actions. A true watchman is motivated by love in everything he or she does. In writing his love treatise, the apostle Paul offered the Corinthian church the following gauge from which to discern true and false workers of the gospel:

> Love suffers long and is kind; love does not envy; love does not parade itself, is not puffed up; does not behave rudely, does not seek its own, is not provoked, thinks no evil; does not rejoice in iniquity, but rejoices in the truth; bears all things, believes all things, hopes all things, endures all things—1 Corinthians 13:4-7.

OUR CHALLENGE TODAY

How will we respond? Will we recognize and confront this counterfeit and destructive voice? Will we deal with our own issues that may blind us or cause us to overreact?

Pastors must arise and lead like Jesus Christ, the bright Morning Star who outshines all other prophetic witnesses and who destroys the works of the evil one. The pastor and the church that seeks to obey God in this matter will be given a greater sphere of authority. Remember:

> Be strong and courageous. Do not be afraid or terrified because the Lord your God goes with you; he will never leave you or forsake you— Deuteronomy 31:6.

Chapter 4

SPINNING THE WEB OF DECEIT

REBECCA WORE AN EMERALD green dress. Although she was not very attractive, Rebecca carried herself seductively. Something about her auburn hair and the way she dressed gained the immediate attention of those around her. As the congregation began to worship, her voice could be heard singing over the others.

Sadly, Rebecca was unaware of what spirit was driving her need to be noticed. In her mind, she was simply trying to live a spiritual life. However, Rebecca had never addressed the wound that created her need for public affirmation. In fact, when confronted with this in the past, she denied any problems in this area. However, her need for recognition saturated everything she did. Thus, she had to be removed from a church staff position.

Rebecca believed the pastor withheld the recognition she truly deserved. Therefore, she began to subtly criticize him as not being spiritual. She asked others to pray that God would cause him to listen to her, because she felt that God had given her insight that would change the church. When this tactic failed, Rebecca looked for other avenues of support. She found a sympathetic ear with the associate pastor.

Demurely, Rebecca began to ask the associate pastor questions with the hidden agenda. He was unaware of Rebecca's motives and how she intended to use his words to rally a grassroots support for her cause. She was planning to overthrow the senior pastor and replace him with the associate pastor. She believed that his sympathetic ear would ensure her further influence and power.

Rebecca began getting bolder in her claims. She used her former church position and began to twist the associate pastor's words, saying the senior pastor was preaching heresy and that he was theologically unsound. She would take the associate pastor's words out of context and insert them strategically into conversation to make it appear as if the associate pastor agreed with her. However, this tactic began to unravel when a counselor approached the pastoral team. Several individuals had confided to the counselor that Rebecca had convinced them the church was becoming cultish. This further fueled their insecurities and fears.

The final straw came when Rebecca, while spreading a lie, was overheard by the associate pastor's wife. Rebecca was saying that the entire leadership team had asked for the senior pastor's resignation. She further claimed the senior pastor had vehemently refused, saying he would never leave the church. Supposedly he was going to publically apologize to Rebecca for dismissing her. When the associate pastor's wife heard all this, she realized what was going on. She shared what she had overheard with the pastoral team.

Slowly, the shroud began to dissipate and each leader realized they had unknowingly turned against the senior pastor after being approached by this woman. The leadership team apologized to the senior pastor for entertaining Rebecca's gossip and becoming ensnared by her web of lies.

What were the woman's characteristics who singlehandedly brought God's judgment on the Church of Thyatira (Revelation 2:20-28)? How could a church—a growing, spiritual fellowship of believers whose deeds were greater than previous years—fall prey to a ploy so grievous to God? How were the pastor and the prophets deceived? Amazingly, the problem was no more obvious to the leaders of the Church at Thyatira than to us today. But as we shall see, those who are influenced by a Jezebel spirit can greatly complicate and confuse many facets of church life, including doctrines and authority issues.

CHURCHES TARGETED BY THIS SPIRIT

No church is too great, too healthy or too pure to be exempted from a Jezebel spirit. In fact, the greater the church, the greater the assurance that those with a Jezebel spirit will seek to gain influence and power—unless the pastor, the leadership team, the intercessors, and those who are prophetically gifted exercise their responsibility and withstand this spiritual attack.

A Jezebel spirit can be found in any type of church or denomination. It is not confined to one particular vein of church affiliation. Although the religious semantics and levels of impact that a Jezebel spirit may exert will differ from setting to setting, the basic characteristics remain the same.

41

Not everyone who succumbs to a Jezebel spirit will set out to destroy their church or to gain power over their pastors and elders. In the beginning, many are simply deceived into believing they are more spiritually sensitive than others. They tend to assume they are always correct. Seldom are they aware that their actions fall into a Jezebelic category.

Certain signs accompany the work of this spirit. Please keep in mind that a single characteristic does not indicate someone has a "full blown" Jezebel spirit. It may simply mean that the person is spiritually and emotionally immature. In this and the coming chapters, I will describe characteristics of the Jezebel spirit. Whenever a combination of three or more of the characteristics exist, there is a strong indication that an individual is being influenced by a Jezebel spirit. (For a more concise list, please see Appendix A.) While one trait may be clearly noticeable, other traits may be unseen. A prolonged manifestation of any of these traits warrants a closer look at the individual and the situation.

The Jezebel spirit works best when coupled with a person who has embraced an Ahab spirit, often found in men. Men can also move in a Jezebel spirit. Some may attempt to join with a work of God at high levels of church government, much like Absalom who appointed himself judge and sat at the city gate meeting anyone who had a grievance. He convinced these people that his judgment would be fairer than his father, David. Absalom would hug and kiss people, thereby stealing the hearts of the people (2 Samuel 15:4-6).

Over the years, I have watched assistant pastors and elders flow in what some have called an "Absalom spirit."

But it is really a masculine form of a Jezebel spirit. In their need to gain recognition and prove they are anointed, they openly or covertly subvert God's appointed authority and engage in lawlessness, thinking they must take action for the sake of the church and the advancement of God's Kingdom. But they secretly go about building their own empire, which is designed to dismantle any other authority.

Conquering the Prophet

Andrea began attending a church that was known throughout the city to be a strong supporter of prophetic gifting. Soon, she began to regularly attend morning prayer meetings. Due to her faithful attendance and presumable prayer life, people began to look to her for advice. Andrea became referred to by many as a "prophet." Flattered by the attention, she subtly encouraged that reputation.

Meanwhile, Andrea searched out all who had prophetic authority in the church. She sought out the senior prophetic voice, asking questions designed to flatter him. She also asked him to mentor her. However, behind his back Andrea began to undermine his abilities and gifts. She spread gossip and questioned his prophetic words for the church. By the time he discovered what was going on, the web had been spun. He was perceived as an "old wineskin" that should be discarded and Andrea became the new prophetic authority.

Disheartened, he left the church. Within two years, the church lost all prophetic and intercessory small groups, and church membership declined from 800 to 250 people. Saying the church had lost its cutting edge, Andrea moved to another church where she repeated her actions once again.

As in Andrea's life, the ultimate goal of someone influenced by a Jezebel spirit involves issues of control and in particular, how disagreements with authority figures are handled. Consequently, any prophetic leader carrying a true spiritual authority from God will be a threat to someone who operates under this spirit.

Since a Jezebel spirit counterfeits the prophetic anointing in gifts, calling, and authority, a prophetic leader will become a target of a Jezebel spirit, as will a church in which the prophetic is held in high regard. A prophetic church and its leaders must realize that if the spirit of Elijah is going to return, so will its counterspirit—the Jezebel spirit.

In its aim to control the prophetic ministry of a church, it also attempts to pervert potential young prophetic voices in achieving their gifting. It seeks to lure them onto a supposed spiritual road that is actually a dead-end, so that they never fulfill the call that God intends for them.

DIVIDE AND CONQUER

The first move a Jezebel spirit will often make is to gain control by trying to remove the established prophetic authority. If a Jezebel spirit can wedge itself between the people, the pastors, and a prophetic leader, then it will move to overthrow the prophetic leader. Discrediting a prophetic leader through reason, strong opinion, and distorted facts are some tools employed by this demonic spirit. Ironically, the person who operates under a Jezebel spirit will have insights that appear spiritual even to those of the pastoral staff.

CONQUER BY JOINING

To seduce, and thereby, conquer a prophetic leader, someone with a Jezebel spirit will seek to gain their favor. This individual will attempt to unite with a prophetic leader in the realm of the spirit, saying "I'm just like you. I seem to know what you're thinking and feeling. We are kindred spirits." However it will be a soulish tie that will attack the prophetic leader's mind, will, and emotions.

This spirit "talks" spiritually, but its strength is born from the power of the soul, and is ultimately deadly to the gifting of its prey. The goal of this demonic spirit is to dilute revelation, bring about corruption, defilement, disregard, and disdain of God's true prophetic voice. In some cases, this eventual joining together will display itself with sexual manifestations.

A Jezebel spirit seeks intimacy with power. It may use fascination and charm in seemingly innocent ways until it gains friendship and confidence—an illegitimate familiarity the person craves. Just as believers are joined by the Holy Spirit, so an individual with a Jezebel spirit will seek to be joined in soul with others under the guise of this union being a spiritual joining.

TIES THAT BIND

You can usually track how godly men or women form a soul-tying relationship with an individual who operates with a Jezebel spirit. It begins in the realm of the soul. Both men and women will find an emotional need being met by this person.

For men, this will often translate into sexual needs and desires. The season of seduction may eventually climax in the act of physical adultery. Thus, their ability to keep a covenant is breached. Their influence and authority is forfeited; their ministry is destroyed and God's Kingdom suffers a great loss. However, if when being enticed and seduced they discern and resist by the assistance of the Holy Spirit, such destruction will be avoided. Scripture tells us that we are tempted to sin when we are drawn away by our own desires and when we allow ourselves to be enticed (James 1:14).

For a female leader, this soul tie will usually manifest as a consuming and magnetic desire to be around the person. They will often become best friends, even soul sisters. The person with the Jezebel spirit may attempt to take over the leaders' group. As the relationship deepens, the leader may feel as if she is being swallowed or suffocated by Jezebel.

A Jezebel spirit creates desire, longing, lust, and an appetite for sin in the heart of a person. When this urge is not restrained, it produces an intense craving. Reasoning will *not* change or halt the demands of this spirit. The individual who becomes enmeshed with this seductive spirit must repent and receive deliverance.

Some individuals with a Jezebel spirit form soul ties by praying and "laying hands on" a prophetic leader, hoping to impart the seed of its spirit. This person may not know they are imparting a demonic touch. They may also want to pray beside a prophetic leader who is ministering to various individuals. They feel compelled to pray for others, but this urge is not from God.

Another ploy is to flatter a prophetic leader. They may present themself as a friend with an understanding

46

ear—a kindred spirit—who knows the pain of being misunderstood and rejected. They manufacture warmth, which entices the prophetic leader to become vulnerable and share personal issues. If a prophetic leader has a weakness of rejection, they can become blinded to a Jezebel spirit that probes his or her weakness in order to gain authority over them. The leader's unmet need to be loved has veiled his or her ability to discern the deception being spun.

A prophetic leader must confront this spirit's attempts to flatter and seduce, whether the seduction is physical or emotional. When challenged, this demonic spirit usually cowers at first in momentary humility. However, it will eventually redouble its strength and rise up like a cobra with great verbal assault. Such volcanic rage can become quite formidable. Once they recognize what is happening, many leaders fail to act and remove themselves from this soul tie. Often the soul tie will make them feel guilty for *not* maintaining the relationship.

Surprisingly, yet of great importance, a prophetic leader must understand that they have *not* been given the authority to overthrow a Jezebel spirit. He or she can only reveal this spirit to their pastor. In Israel, God did *not* ask the prophet Elijah to remove Jezebel. In fact, Elijah exhibited signs of anxiety and depression by sulking and running from her presence. So it fell to Elisha, the next prophetic voice, to forewarn Jehu, who God gave the authority to remove her. Likewise, in Thyatira, God did not ask the prophets to remove Jezebel. He addressed the church pastor. It is the pastor who wields a type of apostolic and kingly authority on the behalf of his flock.

If a prophetic person tries to deal with another person's Jezebel spirit, it simply counterprophesies his or her downfall (1 Kings 19:2). A Jezebel spirit will often cause a prophetic person to run from their responsibility. The prophetic person needs to remove himself or herself from the relationship with Jezebel and seek their own healing.

SUBDUING PASTORAL LEADERSHIP

With her enticing speech she caused him to yield, with her flattering lips she seduced him. Immediately he went after her, as an ox goes to slaughter...He did not know it would cost his life—Proverbs 7:21-23.

The prophetic realm is not the *only* target of a Jezebel spirit. Targeting a pastor and the church staff, a Jezebel spirit will seek to find the weakest link in order to sever it and gain favor in very subtle ways. For a pastor, it will be unbelievable that such a "spiritually mature" person could have anything but the highest of motives.

The more a pastor is blinded to Jezebel's identity, the more likely he or she will fall prey and embrace the "gifted" person. Over time, it will become even more difficult for a pastor to recognize that this individual operates with a controlling spirit that seeks to divide and conquer the pastor.

THE ANOINTING ATTRACTS

Troy had a great anointing from God. Thousands attended the churches he had started and to which he had been given oversight. Mighty signs and wonders followed him. He moved in words of knowledge with incredible accuracy. He was disciplined in prayer, fasting, and was an avid student of Scripture. The magnitude of God's anointing on his life was revealed in his sermons and writings. Even in the early days of his ministry, an apostolic mantle was evident. Yet in ignorance, Troy fell into a trap.

While counseling a woman, he discovered that she was a witch. Without intercessory assistance, he attempted to take her through deliverance. Pretending to be delivered, the witch built a web of flattery, telling Troy how great he was. She claimed that when he prayed, she felt God's touch like never before.

Shortly thereafter, subtle changes began to affect Troy's life. His hunger for spiritual things began to dissipate. His prayer life, fasting, and Bible study diminished. He excused his disinterest as being due to an ever increasing workload. Thus, the trap was set.

After her departure, two other witches were sent by the coven to attend Troy's church and petition Satan to destroy both Troy and his church. These women attended intercessory meetings and began to exert influence on others as they rose to leadership roles. As their influence blanketed the church with deception, they even convinced the intercessors that Troy's wife was a spiritual hindrance to him. Eventually, they "prophesied" that God would take her life so that Troy would become the great man of God he was destined to become.

One of the witches became Troy's secretary. Each day, she made constant innuendoes to him and the staff about his wife's shortcomings. Entertaining the lie that his wife was holding him back, Troy slowly joined with the forces of darkness and agreed that "the Lord should take her home." He began to ask God for an illness unto death to come upon his wife. Troy's wife actually became very ill, but near the point of death, God intervened.

Troy's seductive and vivacious secretary reverted to a new strategy. She hinted that his wife had actually been sent by Satan to keep Troy from producing a godly "man-child seed." As unbelieveable as this sounds, she convinced Troy that she alone carried this golden seed that would be birthed from their sexual union. Enmeshed in the web of deception, the seductive lies had taken root in him. Troy eventually divorced his wife and married this woman. Within nine months, he developed prostate cancer and died. The woman inherited all his wealth. She later drew another pastor into her web and married him. He also died.

From this tragic story, we see how someone with a Jezebel spirit will both love and hate the allure of a pastoral anointing. As light draws a moth, so a pastoral anointing draws a Jezebel spirit. Any power outside its own will threaten a loss of control. This spirit will drive an individual to do anything to gain and maintain control over others. Obtaining a pastor's authority represents the challenge of eating forbidden fruit. A Jezebel spirit is ruthless and deceptive, even to the person who manifests this spirit.

SLOW AND CERTAIN DESTRUCTION

Troy's story is also an example of how someone with a "mature" Jezebel spirit will seek to destroy a man of God through manipulation, deception, and sexuality. This spirit imparts its curse much like the venomous Black Widow spider that destroys its mate after sexual union. Furthermore, with sexual immorality comes a curse of sorcery that results in physical illness and death to the one who joins in this seductive ploy (Revelation 2:22).

When a Jezebel spirit attacks a pastor's wife, the attack may begin to manifest as a barrage of confusing thoughts or as physical or mental illness. The attack may express itself as a physical or an emotional breakdown. When a Jezebel spirit becomes more brazen, it—or a follower who is likewise deceived—will begin to insinuate to others that the pastor's wife is not as spiritual as the pastor. His destiny is being hindered by his wife's lack of spirituality. Obviously, these subversive actions describe the work of a "mature" Jezebel spirit. As this spirit becomes bolder, the person may begin to openly pray that the pastor's wife change or die, in order for the pastor to fulfill God's call.

Surprisingly, an individual with a Jezebel spirit often tries to become part of the church staff. If a position is unavailable, the individual may try to provoke someone to leave or seek their removal from a position. Even more astounding, the individual may brazenly declare to close friends that he or she should have been the pastor, or at least the pastor's wife.

The individual may even suggest they can bear a "godly seed," which could be portrayed as a child or a glorious church. Tragically, when this situation is *not* dealt with, the pastor's marriage often fails and he marries the individual with a Jezebel spirit.

As astounding as this may seem, this scenario is played out around the world scores of times each year. Satan is crafty. Whether it's Naboth's vineyard or a new spouse, a Jezebel spirit will stop at nothing until its goal is obtained. The Church at Thyatira was warned about these very issues. We, too, are warned by the Holy Spirit about these issues still present in the Church today.

Chapter 5

THE SEDUCTIVE FACE OF JEZEBEL

HERODIAS HATED HIM WITH all her heart. Even though he was now in prison, it seemed as if his voice would never be silenced. However, this would soon change. Although her lover was an evil man, he would not order the execution of this prisoner who was esteemed as a prophet. He feared an uprising so she would have to try another ploy.

As much as she hated to admit it, Herodias knew his real lust was for her daughter, Salome. Patiently, she waited to launch her plan on his birthday which the powerful and the influential would attend from around the empire.

On his birthday, Herod was in great spirits. After the wine had greatly fueled his spirit of lust, Herodias approached her daughter. "Go, Salome, dance for Herod. He'll give you anything you ask for and when he does, ask for the head of John the Baptist."

Dressed in a violet tunic that draped her body, the young girl approached Herod and whispered in his ear. He smiled and then asked her to entertain him. As the beautiful young woman begins to dance, her seductive moves enticed everyone in the room, especially Herod. Intoxicated and aroused by passion, he offered to fulfill any wish she had. As Salome looked secretly to her mother, she smiled and said, "I want the head of John the Baptist on a platter." Bewitched by Herodias' beautiful daughter, Herod was putty in the girl's hands.

THE DANCE OF SEDUCTION

The demonic spirit that inspired Herodias to murder John the Baptist (Matthew 14:6-11) was the Jezebel spirit. The spirit of Elijah that rested on John the Baptist had once again threatened and challenged the spirit of Jezebel. Herod, who had an Ahab spirit, was unable to say no to Herodias' demands. In placating her demands, he got what he wanted—sexual favors. She got what she wanted—the death of a prophet who threatened her rise to even greater power and authority.

FALSE FLATTERY

Flattery is a primary tool used by someone influenced by the Jezebel spirit. Flattery is often used to pry open a door to endorsement by a church leadership. Although offering sincere compliments that edify others in the Body of Christ are good, flattery differs in its motive. Flattery seeks to gain approval and recognition by those in authority. Thereby, this spirit only gives in order to get, stealing authority and favor that would rightfully have been given to someone else.

Mistakenly, many pastors believe that a person with a strong prophetic gift automatically possesses the same level of moral character. However, a person operating with a Jezebel spirit—as well as an immature prophetic individual—can portray a very real and sometimes awesome prophetic gift, yet be extremely weak in moral character as well as theology. In someone with a sophisticated Jezebel spirit, flattery will transcend and smooth over any differences between two people. Flattery may be employed to portray profound admiration and endorse the church's vision and direction. Such individuals will speak the same language as the pastor and other leaders, but their motives will be to gain position and control. Stripped down, this is the strategy of "conquering by joining" in spirit.

LAYING A TRAP

As flattery is being bestowed by an individual with a Jezebel spirit, they may tell the pastor about the great things he or she will accomplish, building up false hopes and false expectations about the pastor's future. Once this trap is set, the pastor will be told at precisely timed moments of weakness that there exists a danger to God's plans; someone or something is holding the pastor back. It may be the pastor's spouse, an elder or even another church member. This individual may be heard praying for God to remove a "mystery" person so the pastor "can become all he or she is called to become." They will often guard the identity of the "mystery" person until they are confident of having a strong base of church support. Then, they will reveal the identity of the person who was a threat. This usually results in the person's removal from a position of influence.

54

These destructive maneuvers can bring incredible pressures on a pastor, who is provoked to arise and to prove their worth and anointing to the church.

Pitting One Against the Other

Flattery can also become a catalyst for causing division. Usually this ploy is accomplished through creating destructive "relational triangles." In a triangle, Jezebel will befriend person A and person B. However, she will slowly convince person A that person B does not like them. She will also convince person B that person A does not like them. Jezebel will appear as a peacemaker who has a deep desire to see each one succeed. By playing one person's gifting or wisdom against another's, this spirit produces jealousy, strife, and contention even in the strongest of relationships.

There is no satisfying the endless demands of a Jezebel spirit, because there is always something or someone standing in the way of their quest for power. This drives a pastor to discouragement, defeat, and despair. Over the years, I have watched many pastors retreat to another church rather than fight this battle.

Someone with a Jezebel spirit will seek to gain sympathy from many people, especially when they are confronted. The individual will claim he or she has been spiritually abused. They may use "buzz words" to disarm arguments against them. If a pastor responds defensively to their discourse, he will only reinforce their accusations of being spiritually abused. If a pastor does not have a strong relationship with church leadership, he or she may become trapped in an illogical, unreasonable or senseless catch-22 situation. The following story illustrates this issue.

Kevin, who pastored a small congregation of nearly 100 members began to notice that his worship leader, a man in his late twenties, was taking a lot of liberty during worship. He would often force people to combine various gestures with their praise and worship—dancing or marching around the auditorium. Kevin became troubled because he felt that such expressions should come as a result of the direction of the Holy Spirit, *not* in an attempt to coerce the Holy Spirit to come.

Kevin also observed obvious signs of control and manipulation from the worship leader toward various members of the congregation. On Sunday, the worship leader had publicly challenged Kevin's authority and leadership ability. To complicate the matter, the small church was growing and the worship leader was the only person in the church who could lead praise and worship. Freely, Kevin admitted he couldn't "carry a tune in a bucket."

What was Kevin to do? The worship leader's lawlessness had escalated. Would Kevin have the courage to remove him regardless of the consequences? To do so, Kevin would have to believe in the sovereignty of God. No matter what it would look like initially, the church would become healthier with the worship leader's removal. Thereby, the church would grow correctly.

STRATEGIC AFFILIATION

A Jezebel spirit strategically affiliates with others in the Body that move in spiritual realms. This is usually in an effort to deceive them. A Jezebel spirit realizes that those who are spiritual are looked upon favorably. Therefore, a Jezebel spirit shares that favor through strategic affiliation.

This spirit mounts its campaign to win popular and pastoral endorsement in its bid for growing influence.

The apostles Paul and Silas were on their way to prayer when a woman with this spirit joined them. Simply by walking beside them, she insinuated that she too was going to prayer, hoping to win the acceptance of Paul and Silas and those who watched. She also began to proclaim they were servants of God (Acts 16:16). Pretending to be an intercessor, she attempted to gain a spiritual foothold in the city. Discerning her motives, Paul ended up delivering the woman of a spirit of divination. By strategic affiliation, the demonic plan was to acquire a deeper foothold of influence in the region.

DISMANTLING A WALL OF PRAYER

Robert was the pastor of a growing charismatic church. A woman who had a strong "prophetic" anointing began attending his church.

A few months later, she rose to leadership over several churchwide prayer groups. Unfortunately, the woman began using these groups as a forum to promote her own agenda. Subtly, she began to inject her critical venom about Robert. When he discovered what she was saying, he confronted her. But by then, she had widespread support, having spent hours on the telephone with many church members.

The woman blackmailed Robert with a threat of tearing apart the church unless he acquiesced to her demands. Claiming he was a poor leader, the woman said she was forced "by the Lord" to take the actions she did. In their meeting, Robert became unusually confused and actually ended up agreeing with the woman.

Eight years later when a similar situation occurred, Robert recognized what had happened to him. But by then, it was too late. His church, which had been declining, was now only a handful of people.

Since the tactic of dismantling a wall of prayer is so successful, one objective by someone with a Jezebel spirit is to infiltrate various intercessory groups. Someone with this spirit will try to control the content and direction of prayer. As the person takes over, it is only a matter of time before they become the group's leader. Jezebel spirits usually cause such events by pre-meditated efforts; sometimes the individual is unaware of how their power works. Whether it happens knowingly or unknowingly, the driving force is a demonic spirit.

As the individual plans a takeover, it is not unusual for the current prayer leader to experience sudden or prolonged health problems. They may become confused and lack direction. Eventually, the current leader will resign and right on cue, the individual with a Jezebel spirit will move in and begin to counterfeit true prayer leadership. This sudden role reversal will be accomplished in such a manner that seems natural.

Eventually, false humility and mock timidity will disappear. The individual will begin to declare rather brazenly that they know the mind of God and how everyone should pray. When this happens, it will not be unusual to watch the energy given to prayer increase. Unsuspecting and undiscerning individuals will be tempted to think things are getting better. However, it will not take long for this energy to dissipate. Remember, energy derived from soulish passion will always be short-lived. Only that which is born of the Spirit of God will be maintained by God's Spirit and bear the fruit that remains.

If left unchecked, this takeover will bring an inevitable end to an intercessory group. One-by-one, individuals will be drained of the desire and the grace to pray. The group will begin to dwindle. Thus, the watchmen in God's house will be scattered and the church will be left unprotected. A demonic coup will have taken place. Few will notice the spiritual chill that now blows through the church.

FALSE DREAMS AND VISIONS

When he speaks kindly, do not believe him,
for there are seven abominations in his
heart—Proverbs 26:25.

Tactics intended to frustrate the Kingdom of God will come easy to someone operating with a Jezebel spirit. They seek recognition by trying to manipulate situations to their advantage. From deep within their soul, they will conjure up an unusual number of dreams and visions. They may also "borrow" dreams and revelations that God has given to others, presenting them as if God had given them the revelation. Or they may enhance and embellish their dreams to make them seem even more spectacular and impressive.

Scripture offers an excellent perspective of God's view on this matter.

Therefore behold, I am against the prophets
who steal My words every one from his
neighbor...Behold, I am against the prophets
who prophesy false dreams...and cause My
people to err by their lies and by their recklessness—Jeremiah 23:30-32.

59

CARRYING FALSE BURDENS

This individual will carry false burdens from the Lord, hoping to appear spiritual. He or she may even believe they are speaking God's words, unable to recognize the deception under which they are operating. Once this person gains an open door to the pastor, it is not uncommon for the individual to flood him or her with "revelation" that has supposedly been received from the Lord. Every situation will be subtly manipulated to cast a favorable light on the individual operating with a Jezebel spirit, thus bringing attention to them rather than to the Lord. As this spirit's roots go deeper into the person's soul, righteous and redemptive fruit eventually becomes non-existent.

CREATING SPIRITUAL DEPENDENCY IN OTHERS

The first Sunday she visited, Brian noticed her. He watched her carefree way of meeting people. Secretly, Brian hoped she would demonstrate the leadership qualities he desperately needed due to recent church growth. Brian and his wife, Linda, invited the woman to supper to learn more about her. That evening, Brian did not discover as much as he had hoped, yet the woman seemed confident and able to hear from God. She shared how God had led her to his church. Brian hoped this was a sign of the Holy Spirit's impending move, the very thing for which he had been praying.

In the church services, the woman began giving prophetic words with seeming humility. Her speech was gentle and gracious, mixed with tears. It made her "prophecies" seem from God. But as she became increasingly vocal, giving words Sunday after Sunday, Brian grew uneasy. He also became uncomfortable that the woman was attracting members who were needy, insecure, and spiritually naive. When the woman's husband finally came to church, Brian felt somewhat relieved. Her husband always seemed to be away on business trips.

Everything seemed to go smoothly until four months later. Brian began to notice that several leaders had missed meetings and church services which was uncharacteristic of them. Not long after that, Brian heard rumors that this couple had started a church. Making matters worse, the woman had telephoned church members and urged them to leave Brian's church. Brian was hurt and upset, but what could he do? Should he address it publically? Should he go to the couple privately following the procedure outlined in Matthew 18?

APPEARING MORE SPIRITUAL

When an individual with a Jezebel spirit is put in a leadership position, he or she will try to create an impression of walking on a higher spiritual plane than most. Others may feel less spiritual or intimidated, when they are around this person. This ploy creates emotional dependency in others. Feeling spiritually inferior, they will seek out Jezebel for spiritual guidance. Furthermore, if anyone questions Jezebel's spirituality, they may experience harassment.

New believers are especially prone to this person's subtle, but nonetheless effective, intimidation. Some may choose to pull away from the person, but those who choose to stay will usually comply with Jezebel's demands rather than face being ostracized. Once joined to this spirit, believers who are weak or easily intimidated will find it difficult to remove themselves from the grip of Jezebel.

FALSE HUMILITY

The integrity of the upright will guide them,
but the perversity of the unfaithful will
destroy them—Proverbs 11:3.

Once an individual with a Jezebel spirit receives recognition, they respond initially with false humility. This ploy will serve to further entrap you and convince you of the person's spirituality. However, this misleading meekness will be short-lived. False humility is actually a mask for deeply rooted pride and presumption.

Once this false humility is discarded, the person will proudly offer many "prophetic" promises. Jezebel will foretell of a great kingdom coming to the pastor. However, when these soulish predictions fail to materialize, a pastor's faith is deflated as hope deferred makes the heart sick. An enveloping dark cloud of depression may engulf the pastor, who begins to fight the urge to detach from his or her congregation.

By this time, the person with a Jezebel spirit will have become entrenched in the church. Evicting Jezebel, or curtailing their authority, would bring about an exodus from the church. Even if the pastor knew what to do, he or she no longer could summon the strength to fight back. If the pastor addressed the situation, he or she would risk looking foolish simply because the pastor was the one who placed Jezebel in a leadership position.

EMOTIONAL BLACKMAIL

In leaving—or in threatening to leave—Jezebel will usually discredit the pastor and claim that he or she is not as spiritual as they once had been. Jezebel may also maintain that they are *just* concerned for the people.

At this point, emotional blackmail ensues. Since a Jezebel spirit now holds the key to the emotional balance of the church, the individual will be able to confidently hold the pastor hostage. The pastor, then, becomes captive obeying the directions from a demonic spirit. When this happens, a pastor may sense a sudden "call by God" to leave and shepherd another congregation in a distant city. However, this problem will not disappear until this pastor recognizes and admits to having an Ahab spirit and tolerating a Jezebel spirit.

In the meantime, a similar fate awaits the pastor at the other church. As long as these areas remain unhealed in a pastor's life, Satan will continue to exploit the pastor through an individual who operates with a Jezebel spirit. The reality is that God's severe mercy allows this tormentor to continually plague a pastor until the Ahab weakness is acknowledged, repented of, and healed.

Chapter 6

DEADLY PLOYS

IN THE STAR TREK episode, "A Taste of Armageddon," an alien leader, Anan 7, takes Captain Kirk prisoner. The alien contacts the spaceship, U.S.S. Enterprise, with a voice sounding like Kirk's and orders the ship's shields lowered and everyone on board beamed down to the planet. Upon their arrival, the alien intends to kill them all. Scotty is in command of the ship. When he hears the order, he senses that something is wrong. Scotty asks the computer to analyze the voice. It affirms that the voice came from a voice duplicator and *not* from Captain Kirk.

Like Anan 7, a Jezebel spirit may speak with a prophetic voice that sounds familiar, but, it turns out to be a counterfeit voice. Just as Scotty knew his captain's voice, so believers need to discern the voice of their Commander, the Lord of Hosts, from that of the enemy.

It is difficult to pinpoint how the powers of darkness deceive and counterfeit God's voice or presence. Demonic spirits may sound spiritual. They may even use Scripture to achieve their goals. A discerning ear, however, will detect both accuracy and motive.

In the beginning, a person may start out by saying the right thing in the wrong way. They may believe that God has specifically chosen them, when in fact, their grandiose ideas may stem from a void in their life. In time, they will begin to believe their relationship with God is more spiritual than the relationship others have with the Lord.

The apostle Paul gave this admonition to Timothy:

> Be diligent to present yourself approved to God, a worker who does not need to be ashamed, rightly dividing the word of truth. But shun profane and idle babblings, for they will increase to more ungodliness. And their message will spread like cancer. Hymenaeus and Philetus are of this sort, who have strayed concerning the truth, saying the resurrection is already past; and they overthrow the faith of some—2 Timothy 2:15-18.

In this passage, Timothy is warned to "shun profane and idle babblings" because it will spread like cancer. Although Paul is speaking of people spreading heresy, the same principle can be applied to those operating under a Jezebel spirit. Like those who promote heresy, people who operate under a Jezebel spirit will sow falsehood, division, strife, and discord in "the name of the Lord."

In order to combat this corruption and divisiveness, we must become like Timothy, rightly dividing the Word of Truth. The Greek word used for "divide" in this passage is *orthotomeo,* which means literally to "dissect correctly." Therefore, with the gift of discernment, we can rightly dissect the hidden motives of someone operating under a Jezebel spirit.

DEFENSIVE POSTURING

When confronted with the matters described above, an individual with a Jezebel spirit will usually respond with statements like, "I'm just trying to help," "I'm just following God," or "God told me to do this." Sadly, this response comes more from an imagined sense of God's will. Offering such a response becomes a trump card because by saying that God is the commissioner of the action, it ends all debate. This dead-end logic must not be allowed to rest its case. The battle lies not in the realm of reason, fighting logic with logic. It rests in the realm of the Spirit that divides between soul and spirit.

Tragically, many pastors have found themselves lacking the sharpness to overcome the persuasive arguments of someone with a Jezebel spirit. Many pastors are too busy and distracted by the activities demanded by their congregations. Often a pastor will have little time to spend in the Word and in prayer. Pastors are on-call 24-hours a day, seven days a week. As a pastor, I have experienced and witnessed the enormous demands and pressures placed on these overseers. Eddie and Alice Smith accurately describe this in their book, *Intercessors and Pastors: The Emerging Partnership of Watchmen and Gatekeepers.* Due to family and time constraints, many pastors are unable to discern someone's correct application of Scripture or the spirit of error inspiring its misuse or distortion.

UNREASONABLE AND UNYIELDING

Seeing themselves as spiritually superior, this individual often believes that God has provided a hedge of protection around him or her, isolating them from any deceptive spirit. Sadly, they may even believe they are immune to sin and deception because of their spiritual maturity.

Believing they have been highly favored and chosen for some spiritual high place or position, these individuals conclude that they have a divine, secret strength. Thus, their emotional support comes from within their subjective experience, rather than from God and His written Word.

Eventually, these individuals become unteachable and unyielding. Over time, they will perceive they are infallible. As such, they are unable to listen to others because others have not had a direct revelation from God. Therefore, to reason with them or to question them—so they believe—demonstrates the height of sin and carnality. Such individuals usually demand blind obedience from everyone.

As I teach on this subject, I am always amazed by the number of individuals who share their experiences of following someone with this spirit. They describe how this leader mystically reveals God's supposed plan of action. They are told what to do, when to fast, when to abstain from sexual intimacy with their spouse, and so on. Some are even coerced into praying long hours and giving large sums of money to prove their loyalty.

APPEALING TO OTHERS

There is a way that seems right to a man, but its end is the way of death—Proverbs 14:12.

Seeming to have great spiritual insights into church issues, an individual with a Jezebel spirit usually does not share these insights *first* with the pastor, according to Biblical pattern. Instead, they share their insights about the church with others, building a powerbase of support. Clearly, this is a departure from Scripture. The pattern borne out in Scripture shows that a prophet did *not* go first to the people, but to the king! For it was the king who held the responsibility from God to address and lead the people. The prophet always went directly to the king—not to the people—and God opened the door of access to that realm.

A spirit of rebellion drives this person to take their insights about the church directly to others. Perhaps their revelation comes from a genuine word of knowledge or a word of wisdom. But when the individual oversteps their boundaries, the revelation has become mixed with their soul—the mind, will, and emotions—and becomes corrupted.

Pastors need to notice the little foxes that destroy the vine of their church. Such caretaking will take time, which few pastors have. However until lawlessness is addressed, the leaven will continue to rise until the whole lump—or church—is leavened.

Individuals who give way to a Jezebel spirit do not perceive the value of praying revelation versus speaking it. Deceived by ulterior motives, the individual will appeal directly to others. In doing so, their realm of influence is broadened and the spiritual mysteries they espouse are admired. Thereby, the individual comes to expect honor and adulation from others.

> How can you believe, who receive honor from
> one another, and do not seek the honor that
> comes from the only God—John 5:44.

Alleging mystical insights, an individual with a Jezebel spirit will rarely find things going well in a church. Wanting others to become dependent upon his or her input, the person must prove spiritual maturity that even surpasses that of the pastor. Thereby, Jezebel's followers will keep their eyes upon their new spiritual leader. Consequently, Jezebel will demand to have the "last word" on all church matters.

An individual operating with a Jezebel spirit will generally be tuned to the latest book, tape, or message by various national, spiritual leaders. However, they will distort and take out of context certain elements within a message in order to endorse their own teaching. Thus, the original word or teaching is misused and even laid open to criticism because of how it is erroneously retold.

Brian pastored a large church with one of the strongest Christian schools in the state. One of his intercessory prayer leaders, who is also the mother of two students, had begun to tell several mothers in the school that they were married to the wrong man. She said that for these women's well being and that of their children, they need to divorce their husbands. If they do this, within one year their "God-appointed" soul mates will appear. Several marriages were impacted because of already existing problems in the marriages. The intercessory leader who had gained a "following" had convinced everyone that she was hearing from God.

Often an individual with a Jezebel spirit eagerly seeks to prophetically minister to people, driven by a need for the affirmation of others. They seek out people to proclaim revelation, hoping to gain favor and a devoted following. Mature prophetic voices, on the other hand, seldom seek out people because it drains them immensely. Only when God directs him or her will a mature prophetic individual step forward and minister.

Unfortunately, many who follow someone with a Jezebel spirit will often be new Christians or those naive about spiritual gifts. The naiveté of these believers will be exploited. They will be filled with delusions of grandeur that only occurs if they submit and follow Jezebel. Over time, spiritual strain will often be placed on young or immature believers.

Once they express loyalty, Jezebel will do "an about face." Much like Dr. Jekyll and Mr. Hyde, Jezebel may tell someone about their remarkable spiritual gift that Jezebel alone can develop. Then, as these new followers begin to express their spiritual insight, they are scolded because Jezebel must always maintain the upper hand. Spiritual confusion ensues and replaces healthy spiritual development. This ploy is designed to keep followers dependent on Jezebel, trapped in low self-esteem, and addicted to their leader's teaching and charms.

And many will follow their destructive ways, because of whom the way of truth will be blasphemed. By covetousness they will exploit you with deceptive words; for a long time their judgment has not been idle—2 Peter 2:2-3.

70

Sadly, this experience produces a toxic cycle that eats away at a person's own self worth and leaves naive young believers doubting that God speaks to anyone, including pastors and prophets. Consequently, the true prophetic office that God desires to restore is left suspect to those tainted early in their spiritual walk by the influence of a Jezebel spirit. Whether in the home or in the church, a Jezebel spirit always damages trust in God's true authority.

PRIVATE PRAYER SESSIONS

When it comes to praying for individuals, Jezebel prefers private places. In this way, hurtful innuendoes, implications, and left-handed compliments that are spoken cannot be heard by others or directly challenged. If confronted, this person will usually deny having said anything, or they will insist they were misunderstood. Consequently, it is hard to catch Jezebel undermining a pastor, a prophetic leader, or a church.

It is also quite common for someone with a Jezebel spirit to show up at someone's house without notice, saying the Lord told him or her to go pray for a particular need. This need will often be somewhat elusive and nebulous. There have been times when Jezebel will "invent" a future event that must be stopped. Later, when the invented calamity doesn't manifest, Jezebel will claim their prayers were answered.

Without witnesses, a pastor will have little success trying to verify the specifics mentioned in these private settings. Thereby, Jezebel will elude the evidence that a pastor needs to confront the issue. To establish Jezebel's guilt, a pastor will need two or more witnesses. Usually, if the pastor prayerfully waits and keeps track of specific issues, witnesses will come forward and God will build the pastor's case. Until then, a spirit of confusion will act as a smoke screen and cloud any confrontation made by a pastor. Jezebel will leave the confrontation unscathed while the pastor is left embarrassed and shaking his or her head.

SEEKING OTHERS TO TEACH

"This is the proverbial straw that breaks the camel's back!" thought Steven who had put up with the woman's constant demands to teach questionable material. He could not prove it was scripturally wrong, and based on her righteous appearance and demeanor, Steven had allowed the woman to form a home group for prophetic people.

But now she had crossed the line, mixing Greek mythology with New Age teaching. She claimed that an angel of God had given her "the golden hammer of Thor" to hammer out and forge issues of the Kingdom. Steven wondered how an angel could have given that to her? Why did he let her continue teaching in church circles? Why didn't he stop her two years ago, when she first approached him about teaching others? Now she had her fingers in everything. Pulling her out of leadership roles would be like trying to pry an octopus' tentacles off its prey. There just were not enough hands to go around.

Beneath the woman's soft and gentle demeanor was a mixed-up person who, unfortunately, many considered to be the most spiritual person in the church. A few elders even consider her more pastoral in gifting than the pastor. Furthermore, she was spreading a lie that Steven was only serving as pastor for the money. She claimed that God would remove anyone—including the pastor—who dared come against her. Recently, she approached Steven privately demanding his resignation. How could Steven detach the tentacles of this spirit at this late date without killing his church?

TWISTING SCRIPTURE AND REWORKING DOCTRINES

...there will be false teachers among you, who will secretly bring in destructive heresies—
2 Peter 2:1.

...by her teaching she misleads my servants—
Revelation 2:20.

A person operating with a Jezebel spirit will seek to teach church doctrine in order to gain a controlling grip on the Body. However, their doctrine will be incomplete, inaccurate, and full of holes. Scripture will usually be taken out of context and misapplied. Even if the person's teaching begins correctly, in time it will deteriorate because it has no deep root. Gradually, a slow transition will occur. The Bible will be ignored and mystical ways will take a more prominent role.

Often this person's disciples become confused. Those who are naive will profess allegiance. They will dismiss any questions or concerns initially, thinking they just don't know enough Scripture. Others will wonder: This person seems godly, how could their teaching *not* be from God?

Directly or indirectly, a Jezebel spirit will subtly spread doubts about the pastor, church leaders and other prophetic individuals, especially those who do not endorse Jezebel.

RECKLESS WORDS

Behold, I am against those who prophesy
false dreams, says the Lord, and tell them,
and cause My people to err by their lies and
by their recklessness. Yet I did not send them
or command them; therefore they shall not
profit this people at all—Jeremiah 23:32.

Someone with a Jezebel spirit will seek to gain credibility by speaking prophetic utterances. However, these
prophecies are the product of their own imagination. As
God's spirit begins to lift from them and their reputation
fades, they will take information they know and mix it into
soulish prophesies, telling someone what they want to hear.
The result will be a strange mixture of half-truths with a
powerful allure. For example, obtaining a piece of information from outside sources, Jezebel will announce it to the
pastor as if it were a prophetic word. Subsequently, when it
comes to pass, Jezebel will appear to be a true prophet. This
practice is very manipulative and deceptive, and God hates it!

Likewise, an individual with a Jezebel spirit will
prey on a pastor's poor memory. Because the pastor does not
clearly remember word-for-word what was said, Jezebel will
twist or give "new" meaning to their previous prophecies.
Thus, they will ensure that all of their prophesies are totally accurate. This person is not looking for accountability.
Consequently, they will tend to be evasive and abrasive to
truth, and dislike any demands for accuracy and accountability. Rarely will they admit an error. However, they will
concede only to survive and fight another day.

On the other hand, men and women with a prophetic calling will welcome accountability and demonstrate mutual submission as they grow in godliness. They will concede to making mistakes because they understand that a prophetic gift matures with time.

FALSE PROPHECY

Giving a false prophecy does not simply mean speaking an untrue word. It may mean that a false, lying, and unclean spirit is speaking through a person who is giving a prophetic word.

Instead of revelation, the Jezebel spirit uses a spirit of divination, which in the Greek is literally called *python*. Much like the woman with a spirit of python in Acts 16:16, Jezebel's theology may contain accurate insight. Yet, an unclean spirit operates through the person.

Usually, it takes great discernment to discover which spirit is speaking—the Holy Spirit or the unholy spirit. An immature or unsuspecting hearer will not be able to discern the difference. A mature prophet can discern a Jezebel spirit, thus "separating the holy from the profane" (1 Corinthians 14:29; Ezekiel 44:23). Remember, the hallmark of the Holy Spirit is always purity, truth, and sincere love.

EAGERNESS TO IMPART

For I long to see you, that I may impart to you some spiritual gift, so that you may be established—Romans 1:11.

Counterfeiting the doctrine of the laying on of hands (Hebrews 6:1-2), a Jezebel spirit likes to impart its anointing through the laying on of hands. However, Jezebel's touch carries a curse. Ask yourself: If it is *not* the touch of God, then what spirit is touching you?

When a Jezebel spirit is imparted, a dark spirit is deposited into its victims. Obviously, an individual with a Jezebel spirit is *not* someone that you want to have ministering to people in a prayer line! Even if the person is unaware of Jezebel operating through them, they are still capable of passing on this demonic spirit to others.

Their impartation may result in what appears as a healing, as demons of affliction are shifted from organ to organ. Or, Jezebel may want to pass on a "higher" level of spiritual anointing. They may claim their higher anointing can break through walls or chains that have held back an individual or a pastor. They may even claim that God has told them to do this.

Such individuals are presumptuous to think they have this level of authority, because, in essence, they are declaring to be greater than their pastor. Imagine trying to impart something you have to your pastor in order to increase his greatness. Such thinking is twisted. According to Scripture, it is always the greater who blesses the lesser (Hebrews 7:7). In the end, an individual's motive distinguishes godly prayer from soulish, manipulative, and carnal prayer. The hidden motive behind such prayer is to increase recognition and elevation for Jezebel.

Praying for your pastor is necessary and should be practiced on a regular basis. In fact, forming a prayer shield around a pastor is essential to win today's Kingdom battles. Once again, I recommend the book, *Intercessors and Pastors: The Emerging Partnership of Watchmen and*

Gatekeepers that offers suggestions for appropriate boundaries between intercessors and pastors.

APPEARING RELIGIOUS

> Take heed that you do not do your charitable
> deeds before men, to be seen by them—
> Matthew 6:1a.

Individuals with a Jezebel spirit will exhibit a religious spirit. He or she may appear to be the most spiritual person you have ever known. They may portray that they have a deep and intimate relationship with the Holy Spirit. However, a closer inspection will reveal their actions are based on what they think you need to see, to convince you of their spirituality. Perhaps this person will be the first to cry, wail, or mourn, claiming a burden from God. But such behavior will simply be a ruse, meant to promote the individual in the eyes of others.

Often, this person will let many people know they have spent hours in prayer or in fasting. Or, that they gave all their money away. The "righteous" deeds of someone with a Jezebel spirit are always done for everyone to see. These actions only serve to promote and to enlarge the kingdom of self.

Believing they are a "special instrument" of God, such individuals often isolate themselves from others and take a separate path, feeding their independent spirit. A religious spirit blinds them to the sober knowledge of the deception they have bought into. Like a tidal wave, deception floods the mind, deepened by the continual need for sensual—even sexual—stimulation. Thereby, some individuals will begin to view communion with God as a sensual thing. In ignorance, they may begin to commune with evil spirits, and eventually claim that God has entered their body as in a sexual union. They will privately tell others they have actually become the "bride" of Christ. They will even begin to experience physical undulations of a sexual nature, thinking they are giving themselves to the Holy Spirit, just as Mary did.

EXPERIENCES ARE DRAMATIZED

It is common for someone with a Jezebel spirit to entertain a strange mixture of Christianity, New Age, and eastern religions. Their actions and religious displays are meant to convey many mystical experiences and impress others sufficiently so that they will be accepted in the way they deeply desire. Jezebel's actions will be overly exaggerated. Their vocabulary and orations will become unnecessarily dramatized. As this spirit matures, a person's voice may change when giving a prophetic word. Sometimes an unnatural voice will be manifested, as if the vocal inflection proved that God was with them. This is no different than channeling, as a spirit—not the Holy Spirit—uses the individual's vocal chords.

Although every man or woman of God has a sense of destiny and purpose, this divine purpose should *not* be confused with a Jezebel spirit's false spirituality. Where God's purposes in our lives lead to humility, Satan's purposes in our lives cultivate self-promotion. Often, the intent of the heart is the initial dividing line between the two.

Family Life in Disorder

Often, instability exists in the family life of someone plagued by a Jezebel spirit. This spirit will breed negative attitudes, behavior, and individuals. Families can be destroyed by this spirit. Individuals who operate in this spirit can be single or married. If Jezebel is married, their mate will be spiritually weak, miserable, or unsaved. They can also operate in the same spirit.

Scripture says that before we can be in any type of leadership, our family must be in order, our children in good standing, and our mate in one accord with us (1 Timothy 3:1-4). How can you have a prophetic spirit to restore families (Malachi 4:6), if your own family is destroyed or in disarray? You cannot impart what you do not have. Furthermore, you have no authority to impart that which you did not build.

Often, the husband of a woman who operates with a Jezebel spirit will not be able to stand as the priest of his household because a Jezebel spirit will destroy the family priesthood, just as Jezebel destroyed Jehovah's priesthood and emasculated King Ahab. Their mate often becomes lazy, sluggish, and repressed. The husband allows his wife to dominate and control him, but secretly he despises and hates her for it. As she becomes more aggressive, he becomes more reclusive. Sexual intimacy between them takes a back seat to her spiritual needs. He quietly begins to search for other means of meeting his needs. Out of anger, he may turn to flirtatious acts, pornography, cyber-sex, voyeurism, or other ways to alleviate his relational pain and make himself feel good and in control.

Some husbands and wives will both operate in a Jezebel spirit. When this happens, it becomes a formidable match as their demonic spirits work in unison. However, much like a Queen Bee, the woman will continue to retain the upper hand. The husband, even if he appears to be strong, will be her slave. His duty in looking strong is to make her look even better.

If Jezebel's husband is a believer, this spirit will cause a man to forsake his priestly, God-given responsibilities as the spiritual leader of his home. In some cases, the husband may offer some spiritual nourishment. He may even lead family devotions. Such actions are allowed by Jezebel so that others—or even himself—are unable to recognize her veiled control. But, in reality, she continues to hold the real authority in their home. Aware of the biblical teaching on divine order in marriage, she may decide not to demonstrate her power openly when friends visit. However, her control will be reinforced when she is alone with her husband.

An individual with a Jezebel spirit will often maintain control over her husband through the marriage bed. She rewards his obedience with sexual gratification. When her husband rebels, she withholds sexual intimacy.

LOOKING TO OTHER MEN

She may claim that she wants her husband to assume the spiritual leadership of their family. And if he did, she would submit to him. Yet, if the earlier scripting has been etched on the husband's soul, nothing will change.

She may coerce the pastor to intervene and act as the head of their household. However, if she is not submissive to her husband, she will not be submissive to the pastor or to

God. It is just a matter of time until the pastor, too, feels the sting of her emasculating jabs.

Her husband's weakness may cause a wife to be drawn to and spend time with other men who demonstrate spiritual headship, thus filling a void in her marriage. Eventually, her husband will become so demoralized that he will cease going to church, preferring to stay home watching television, playing sports, or engaging in other substitutes for his wife's affection. After all, how can he listen to a pastor who can't see through his wife's spiritual facade?

CASTRATING HER HUSBAND

A Jezebel spirit will influence a woman to criticize and belittle her husband, telling him he's not spiritual enough, bold enough, making enough money, or that he's holding her back from the ministry God has awaiting her. She may apply subtle, manipulative pressure on him by simply sighing and commenting how nice it would be to have this or that, knowing they can't afford it. She may also imply that if he really loved her, he would work harder to provide for all her needs and desires. Such manipulative ploys will put incredible pressure on a man and increase his resentment. It may also cause him to flee into the arms of another woman who is more sensitive to his needs.

In God's order, the authority over the wife is the husband, the authority over the husband is Christ, and the authority over Christ is God the Father (1 Corinthians 11:3). A person with a Jezebel spirit will talk about submission and obedience to her husband, but both her husband and children know that it's all talk. It is *not* reality.

81

Children who grow up in a family environment where a parent operates with a Jezebel spirit will be profoundly affected as an adult, in ways many do not realize. While I am not a psychologist or an expert on childhood issues, I have noticed through hundreds of encounters, interviews, and testimonies that the following results are the ones most often encountered.

IMPLICATIONS FOR DAUGHTERS

Daughters reared by a domineering mother may manifest masculine or overtly aggressive behavior. Becoming like their mother, they repress their true femininity and regard it as a detriment. For some, seeds of rebellion, manipulation, and control have been sowed into their hearts by a domineering mother. They, in turn, may begin to operate with a Jezebel spirit. Blind to the true source of their pain, some will embrace the women's rights movement or a goddess movement like Wicca. Sadly, even if a young woman longs for a man to step in and fill the void left by her father, she may find it hard to trust men as well as God the Father.

IMPLICATIONS FOR SONS

Whenever parents are not fulfilling their rightful roles in marriage, their sons will become confused about their masculinity. Some may become sexually aggressive and seek to subdue women by force. Young men may also respond to their mother's browbeating by becoming overbearing tyrants, and thereby, seek to dominate their wives and children. Male subjugation of women is often motivated by a resentment against a domineering mother figure.

Some young men may express their resentment toward women and overreact by running from women. They may respond to their unfulfilled need for a father's affection and authority by being attracted to the same sex, particularly if he eroticizes the masculine void in his life.

When Warren was 18 years old, he had prophetic gifts that were being touted as extraordinary by nationally known leaders. Even as a young man, Warren had been taken to the Third Heaven. He could tell you with amazing accuracy when you would be visited by an angel or give you a date something would happen and it would come to pass. However, Warren had a secret obssession. Although many women found him attractive, Warren was deeply attracted to men.

This attraction began when Warren was 9 years old. His mother pastored a pentecostal church. His father, who was cold and distant, took little interest in the church, the family, or in Warren. When an evangelist came to town to hold his yearly meetings in their church, Warren noticed his mother's attraction to this man.

The evangelist, who recognized Warren's prophetic abilities even at this young age, approached Warren's mother about the young boy traveling with him during the summer months. He wanted to train Warren. She was thrilled. It was during this time, however, that Warren was sexually molested by this man.

When Warren told his mother, she refused to believe him. Warren always suspected that his mother's inability to believe him stemmed from his belief that his mother was having an affair with this evangelist. A strong and domineering woman, she dismissed Warren's pain and accused her son of lying. Tragically, Warren never recovered from this incident or his mother's anger toward him.

Since Warren's father was emotionally distant and unavailable, the visiting evangelist began to fill the masculine role model in Warren's life. Although Warren fought his homosexual tendencies, he was always looking for a man to replace his father. His anger toward his mother further fueled his attraction to men.

As Warren's prophetic gift was recognized, he would have periodic sexual liaisons followed by long periods of anguished repentance and abstinence. Each time, the Lord would return the anointing to Warren. Then while ministering in a foreign country, Warren became ill and was unable to recover. He was sent home and was later diagnosed with AIDS. Warren died at age 32.

Chapter 7

UNCOVERING THE ROOTS

KORAH AND HIS FOLLOWERS had been planning to launch a revolt for quite some time. It was evident that Moses and Aaron were old and feeble. Their leadership had only brought further wandering in the desert! Korah and his fellow Levites had continued to challenge Moses and his ridiculous demands. Looking across the great congregation, Korah felt confident that Israel would be stronger under his leadership. Someone like himself must arise and oppose the old man. Suddenly, Korah heard a voice cry out. It was the voice of Moses.

"Depart from the tents of these wicked men!" Moses cried out to those standing near Korah. "Touch nothing of theirs or you will be consumed by their sin!"

As people began backing away, Korah and his family—as well as his followers and their families—stood at the door of their tent. What was Moses up to now?

As he faced the congregation, Moses began to shout, "By this you shall know that God has sent me to do these works, for I have not done them of my own will! If these men die naturally like everyone else, then the Lord has not sent me. But if the Lord causes the earth to open its mouth and swallow them up with all that belongs to them and they go down alive into the pit, then you will understand that these men have rejected the Lord" (Numbers 16:28-30).

As soon as Moses finished speaking, Korah felt a tremor beneath his feet. Suddenly, the earth split apart beneath him. He, his family, and all their belongings fell into the pit. Then the ground closed over them. Although it all happened in a matter of seconds, Korah must have felt the horror of knowing he was about to die and that he had come under God's judgment. Those around them fled, trampling over one another, fearing that God's judgment would touch them, too. Without warning, a strange fire came out of Heaven and consumed the 250 followers of Korah.

1. A ROOT OF REBELLION

Thinking he was right in his assessment of Moses' leadership, Korah exalted his will above that of Moses. Likewise, Jezebel will believe its assessment of a pastor's leadership and attempt to launch a revolt. Since God places all authority in their position, a revolt against that authority is rebellion—lawlessness—against God. (I will say more on the spirit of lawlessness in Chapter 9.)

For those operating in a Jezebel spirit, rebellion is at the core of their being. Thinking they have heard from God, they exalt their will above God's will or above the authority God has placed over them (Hebrews 13). Whenever our will is served by our desires, we are worshipping our self-interests, not God's. We, in essence, have become our own idol.

God equates rebellion with witchcraft, which is power gained by the assistance of evil spirits (1 Samuel 15:23). It makes little difference whether an individual is cognizant of the evil spirits influencing him or her.

In Scripture, Jezebel was distinguished by witchcraft (2 Kings 9:22a). So, it should not be surprising that a Jezebel spirit operates through witchcraft, even in the early stages of this spirit's rule in someone's life.

IMPOSING ON OTHERS

The spirit of witchcraft imposes its will by manipulating others. Raping the value of each individual, witchcraft bypasses an individual's decision-making capabilities and establishes its own "higher" authority at the expense of its victim. It may involve an expression of illegitimate authority that has been usurped. It may also involve an unrighteous expression of legitimate authority. For instance, a pastor may use his or her authority unrighteously by manipulating others in the Body.

At the heart of such actions is an attitude of irreverence—devaluing an individual who is made in God's image. This spirit also portrays disrespect for the preciousness of the human will. God gave us the gift of free will and God Himself does not violate it.

Manipulating others does not make an individual a witch—someone who has covenanted with Satan. Nor does it mean the individual is a practitioner of magic, hexes, potions, and incantations. But it suggests that a person is masking their true intention. Jezebel allows others to become sacrificial pawns to accomplish its plan. Its follow-ers are simply convinced Jezebel is right and the pastor is wrong. Initially, most believe by imposing their will, they are only endeavoring to build the Kingdom. They are not in touch with their own issues that blind them to what God is doing. Those who practice manipulation in their homes and in personal relationships will do the same in church set-tings, unless the error is corrected. In order for a church to flourish, contol and manipulation must cease.

THINGS DONE IN SECRET

In Scripture, the word most often used for witchcraft is the Hebrew word *anan,* which means to cover or to act covertly. This is exactly what the Jezebel spirit does.

Although an individual may not be a practicing witch, nor a mature Jezebel spirit with the aim of destroy-ing a church or pastor, he or she may still have a spirit of witchcraft. A person can be a Christian and operate in witchcraft without even realizing it. This spirit has long been hibernating in the Body of Christ and sadly, it operates through some of the Lord's chosen vessels. Even mature prophetic or intercessory individuals can periodically oper-ate under the influence of this spirit if there are doors that remain open through old wounds. Evidences of these wounds not being healed would be if the individual strug-gles with feeling overlooked, undervalued, or rejected. Or if they struggle with bitterness, criticalness, and anger.

For example, Terry and Lisa were active in church for their entire fourteen years of marriage. Terry had a great job in telecommunications and Lisa loved staying at home with their children. Terry was a good man. He just wasn't passionate about spiritual growth. Playing golf on Sunday was more relaxing than attending church.

Lisa had sought to obey God, but it always seemed to result in misunderstandings, dashed hopes, and eventual pain. It seemed that every church they attended had major problems. They always seemed to find themselves right in the middle of the fray.

Sobbing at the kitchen table, Lisa could not understand why they have been asked to leave the church. They were only trying to help people. After all, she could not help it if she "sees" what others do not. The pastor could be a great man, but he would not listen to her. If only he would. Many stood beside her. Why didn't the pastor? The person overseeing the prophetic ministry was totally against her. Still, Lisa had managed to become the assistant prayer leader and oversaw seven of the fourteen prayer groups. She dreamed one day of leading them all.

Since childhood, Lisa had always wanted to be a pastor. If given the right situation, she would lead the church through intercession. She would make their prayer ministry the largest in the state. She would be key to the pastor's success. With her strategic know-how and his authority, they could have built the largest church in the city. Missionaries would have been sent to the nations and hundreds of prophets would have been trained with the new training program that she longed to implement. It was a shame that someone's petty jealousy had stopped her.

As Lisa listened to herself, she noticed anger and bitterness spewing out of her mouth. "Why not?" she argued with herself. She had been wronged again. She knew Terry would simply shrug his shoulders and give her a token response, "I'm sorry." Lately, she had wondered if their marriage would make it. Sometimes she wondered if she had married the wrong man.

Lisa does not know it, but she has already embraced the first level of pride and self-promotion that will lead her down the road to greater deception by a Jezebel spirit.

One of the initial evidences of a Jezebel spirit influencing a person is how they handle disagreements with authority figures. It is not wrong to disagree with a leader; it is what you do with the disagreement that may be Jezebellically inspired. We must follow proper protocol for conflict resolution as outlined in Scripture (Matthew 18). We also need to consider the examples of Esther and Haman, David and Saul.

SELF-CENTERED BEHAVIOR

Like Lisa, a believer influenced by a Jezebel spirit may not intend to destroy a church. However, individuals who operate in varying levels of rebellion and witchcraft have destroyed many churches. Thus, witchcraft is able to work through an individual who tries to take control.

Manipulative control is strengthened with each successful endeavor. Full of self-pity and pride, an individual's soul is endangered by deeper demonization. This type of witchcraft can be performed without occult involvement, even by Christians who profess Jesus as their Lord. A person who operates in a more mature form of witchcraft is determined to impose their will, no matter what the moral cost. In the case of Jezebel, her use of manipulative control resorted to murder.

Not only is witchcraft displeasing to God, it hinders relationships in which honesty is vital. Since witchcraft violates the will of others and their ability to choose, it greatly damages a husband-wife relationship. It is also destructive in parent-child relationships and relationships with other family members. In situations where conflict arises, individuals who operate in this spirit refuse to communicate truthfully, and sometimes not at all. Furthermore, they will employ artful, unfair, or insidious means to gain an advantage and achieve their goals, thinking their cause justifies their actions.

Today, God is crying out for godliness and righteousness to arise. When God appoints leaders, it is a prophetic statement that He intends to advance His Kingdom on Earth. Therefore, every advance comes through God's appointed leaders. A Jezebel spirit will seek to abort God's advance by usurping the rule of pastors and leaders.

The summons to take dominion and authority in the Earth is *not* a call for oppressive domination. Domination is actually a fleshly substitute for the godly exercise of ordained authority.

2. A ROOT OF BITTERNESS

> ...looking carefully lest anyone fall short of the grace of God; lest any root of bitterness springing up cause trouble, and by this many become defiled—Hebrews 12:15.

Rebellion, in all its forms, has several roots, one of which is bitterness. Bitterness opens a door by which a Jezebel spirit slithers into a person's soul undetected. Bitterness often takes hold in our lives when we feel we are being overlooked for recognition or honor. Self-pity sets in and a person, knowingly or unknowingly, begins to seek ways of getting attention to display the gift they believe they have.

Bitterness resides in our soul, because it is a mental stronghold linked to selfishness and pride. Bitterness may be directed toward God or anyone whom God endows with authority. Since bitterness often is a reaction to a perceived injustice or to unjust authority, it will provoke a person to react against all authority, whether just or unjust. Bitterness brings despair. But since bitterness is tied to pride, this despair will drive a person to design schemes that promote their gift.

Bitterness is truly sinful. It deeply damages an individual and leads to lawlessness. As with all sin, bitterness must be recognized, repented of and healed through God's grace.

SOUR FRUIT

A root of bitterness will produce varied fruit. It may birth immorality (Hebrews 12:14-16), lifelong anger and resentment, or a pattern of broken relationships. Moreover, a root of bitterness is contagious. A bitter spirit will infect the spirit of many others.

The Cross is the turning point for this bitter root. Jesus alone is the Great Physician who can deliver us from demonic torment. His anointing can turn us from our rebellious ways. Thus, a bitter, rebellious heart can be transformed into a grateful, obedient heart, as it is touched by the grace of God. After such deliverance, the person must decide to submit to God-given authority. Submission is a decision—rather than a feeling—which an individual makes. A continual practice of submission will produce meekness. Remember, Jesus said that the meek will inherit the Earth (Matthew 5:5).

3. A ROOT OF BONDAGE

> For you did not receive the spirit of bondage
> again to fear—Romans 8:15a.

A root of bondage leads to fear and produces a spirit of legalism, depression, servitude, enslavement, and control. Someone enslaved to a Jezebel spirit—either as its vessel or as its victim—cannot taste true liberty.

Scripture says that wherever the Spirit of the Lord is, there is freedom (2 Corinthians 3:17). Freedom brings about responsibility and accountability. Yet, those who operate with a Jezebel spirit will welcome responsibility, but not accountability. They will perceive accountability as slavery and avoid it like the plague.

Often individuals in the grip of this spirit are unable to sense their adoption as a son or a daughter of God. They feel isolated and uncared for. While striving to meet their own needs, they embrace a victim mentality because life "owes" them something. Even if given an extravagant gift, they exude a lack of gratitude, feeling they deserve whatever was given to them. In fact, they always feel as if more should have been given to them.

4. A ROOT OF FEAR

> For the thing I greatly feared has come upon
> me, and what I dreaded has happened to
> me—Job 3:25.

Fear, which is a lack of faith, opens the door for a Jezebel spirit to enter an individual's life. A mindset of fear may begin in childhood. It then continues until an individual's soul gains rule and begins to control them. A spirit of fear—

a mental stronghold of the soul—may lie to a young girl. It will whisper, "I will protect you. I will be your refuge from other people's domination. I will give you control." This spirit's deception happens subconsciously because it bypasses cognitive understanding and goes directly to influence an individual's actions. Thus, a spirit of fear causes you to learn to react to situations with fear.

A spirit of fear always gains its influence during our weakest moments. These moments usually follow on the heels of an episode in our life that has left deep scars on our psyche. They can also arise from spoken fears of our parents and others. Unfortunately, many well-meaning parents use fear to control a child, rather than develop a child's ability to make wise choices.

By the Spirit of God, a root of fear can be removed. It can only be accomplished by those willing to pay the price of prayer, patience, and forbearance. They must desire to forgive any authority figure who has wounded or abused them.

MENTAL STRONGHOLDS

Lies spoken by seducing spirits are *very* subtle. They arrive as thoughts "spoken into a soul" by a cunning and shrewd evil spirit. At first, the thoughts seem logical and just. Once they are embraced, believed, and accepted, these thoughts become deeply embedded into our subconscious mind. They become a way of thinking, or in other words, a mental stronghold. Your conscious mind may never knowingly process the thoughts that enter it from that point on, unless you receive revelation from God and discern that a demonic spirit is trying to control your thoughts.

94

Most strongholds take root during our childhood years. Generally speaking, your parents probably did not have the discernment to nullify such attacks of spiritual warfare. For those parents who were able to discern a lying spirit, often they were not adequately versed in the Word of God to teach their children how to defend themselves against such attacks. Consequently, we have all become potential prey for Satan's lying snares (2 Timothy 2:25-26).

To agree with a lying spirit is to become its prisoner. Such dishonest spirits are demanding prison guards. The same spirit that works *through* and *for* them also works *against* them, to keep a person from escaping. In a twisted way, these demonic prison guards will try to convince an individual that their prison cell is actually a vehicle that will bring about their long-awaited position of honor. But it is an illusion.

Whenever we accept the enemy's lies, we then willingly accept rejection, insignificance, and insecurity. We begin to doubt having a loving heavenly Father. Consequently, a stronghold of fear will produce untold anxiety and depression (Proverbs 12:25).

Once a person is able to recognize these strongholds, they can find true freedom. Removing a spirit of fear will sever a major root of the Jezebel spirit. Freedom and inner healing for past wounds are accomplished by renouncing a false trust in an evil source and by receiving a renewed trust in the Lord Jesus. More will be said about this in Chapter 12.

5. A ROOT OF PRIDE

Mystery, Babylon the great, the mother of harlots and of the abominations of the earth—Revelation 17:5.

> ...for she says in her heart, 'I sit as queen,
> and am no widow, and will not see sorrow'—
> Revelation 18:7.

Pride is the tap root of a Jezebel spirit. Pride involves lifting or elevating yourself in order to rule in stature or influence. A spirit of pride is contrary to the Holy Spirit.

Mary, the mother of Jesus, is a good example of the antithesis of pride. When the angel Gabriel announced that she would bear the Savior of the world, she pondered over the mystery of why the Lord chose a humble maiden for such an awesome destiny (Luke 1:46-55). The spirit of pride is also unlike the heart of Esther, who humbly entreated her authority to hear her petition. Because of her meekness, her cries were heard and a nation was saved. Nor is this spirit of pride typical of Deborah's heart. As a prophetess and a judge of Israel (Judges 4:4-9), Deborah did not want to presume or wrongfully take leadership that belonged to another. Instead, she stepped into leadership *only* at the insistance and invitation of the leader.

ACTIVE WAITING

Anna had just finished lighting the last candle in the temple. The autumn chill had come earlier this year. But on this morning, the cool air seemed particularly refreshing and her prayers seemed alive and unhindered. Perhaps it was the fast she had just ended. But soon, Anna knew she would see the Light of Israel and of the world.

Years ago the Lord told her in a vision that if she would pray for the coming of the Messiah, she would live to see His arrival. Since her husband had died, Anna had set her heart to serve the Lord daily—from morning until evening—for the past fifty seven years. At times, it had been hard to keep going, but the Lord had helped her. People kindly brought her provisions. How could she not serve Jehovah Jireh? He truly provides!

Across the couryard, she saw Simeon coming to say his prayers. Today, he arrived earlier than usual. She watched as he knelt and raised his hands toward Heaven. The intense presence of the Holy Spirit was in the Temple. Walking around the porch area near the altar, Anna fell to her knees sobbing great tears. God's presence was so powerful. When she arose and walked toward the courtyard to pray for others who would come that morning, she gasped as she passed one of the huge pillars that held up the temple's roof.

Simeon was speaking with a rugged looking young man and his beautiful young wife—both were radiant. As Simeon took their little baby in his arms, tears flowed down his face and beard. When he lifted up the child to bless him, Anna knew in her spirit that Simeon was holding the Redemption of Israel. As Simeon began to prophesy over the child, Anna was led by the Holy Spirit to go throughout the temple proclaiming God's promise was fulfilled. The Messiah had come!

For nearly sixty years, Anna served in the temple with meekness, contrition, and steadfastness (Luke 2:36-38). Self-promotion was not evident in her life. Others called Anna a prophetess, but she did not. As a result, God exalted her.

DESPISING MEEKNESS

Jezebelic pride is the antithesis of humility. In Scripture, Jezebel is portrayed as glorifying herself and living luxuriously. Full of presumption, she decided to "sit as queen" (Revelation 18:7). This arrogant spirit will despise the lowly estate of a widow or of any woman. This puffed-up spirit views meekness and humility as inherently worthless and debase. As such, this spirit despises subordination to authority because to be submitted to authority would require a sacrifice too great to offer.

Instinctively, this haughty spirit uses seductive qualities to lure others into their schemes. Desperate for attention, they desire the infatuation and idolatry of men, who are then led to their death.

A SEXUAL TEMPTRESS

Several years ago I listened in amazement as David shared what had happened to him. He seemed to have the perfect life: a beautiful wife and a job that he loved. His church was bursting at the seams. David was frequently in the newspapers. Everything seemed to be coming together for David, except in his marriage. It had been months since he and his wife had been sexually intimate. Their marriage was becoming strained. He kept planning to take some time off from work.

David began noticing other women. Even after seeing them in church, he found himself fantasizing about them. One woman in particular caught his attention. David was pleased to see her name scheduled in his calender one day. Feeling more excited about seeing her than he should have been, he decided to cautiously guard his emotions.

The appointment went smoothy. The woman seemed vivacious and eager to serve. She secretly told David that her attractiveness had been a disadvantage in other churches. Two weeks later, she returned again. This time, she was wearing a full length fur coat. At the time, it didn't seem strange since it was beginning to turn cold outside. As she entered David's office, he closed the door, as was his usual practice since his secretary's desk was just outside. Standing in the middle of the room, the woman began to tell David how anointed he was.

She shared a vision of him preaching to kings and presidents, and she wanted to help him get there. She revealed that God had given her some insight. Looking into his eyes, she told him that she was aware he and his wife had not been intimate in a while. She knew his loneliness. Appealing to his pride, she said that David and other great men of this age were like "King David." Her role was to help the king in any way she could. Just as it was for David and Solomon, one woman could not satisfy the sexual needs of a man with such a great calling.

Intoxicated by her tantalizing words and sensuality, David stopped breathing for several seconds. Then in a bold move, the woman dropped her fur coat revealing her nakedness. His heart pounding with anticipation, a powerful seduction came over him. Moving around the side of his desk, David touched her and gave into the craving that had gone unmet for so long.

During the sleepless nights that followed, waves of shame and guilt washed over David. He wanted to run, to turn back the clock, and erase what had happened. Eventually, David resigned from the ministry. His three thousand-seat church building was later sold at an auction.

I find more bitter than death, the woman whose heart is snares and nets, whose hands are fetters. He who pleases God shall escape from her, but the sinner shall be trapped by her—Ecclesiastes 7:26.

The pride of our anointing can be the seed to our eventual downfall. It can also lead to a fatal attraction.

THE COMING DECEPTION

Nearly 2,500 years ago, the prophet Zechariah described a spirit of pride that would hide behind a coming deception involving women. I believe he was shown a vision of the Jezebel spirit arising in the Earth today (Zechariah 5:5-11). Zechariah saw a basket that was divided into six parts. The number six is the number of man, depicting fleshly effort. When the basket cover was raised, Zechariah saw a woman sitting inside. When the woman tried to escape, an angel forced her back into the basket and placed a lead weight over the cover. Then, two women with wings like a stork, took the basket to the land of Shinar or Babylon, where this woman would sit on a lofty pedestal. The Lord called this woman, who was a demanding and prideful spirit, "Wickedness."

Today, women who strive for power, position, and rule will often unsuspectingly embrace an Antichrist spirit. This spirit will urge, push, and cajole women to demand position and authority, much the way the women's rights movement has operated in our day. Thus, these women will fall into the snare of Babylon.

A spirit of pride will make it very difficult for this individual to repent. The person will need to realize that humility before God is priceless. They will need to give up a defensive posture against authority and usurping the authority of another—particularly male authority. If they repent of a spirit of pride, they will be spared a great and hideous deception.

Rooted in Our Spirits

...beloved, let us cleanse ourselves from all
filthiness of the flesh and spirit, perfecting
holiness in the fear of God—2 Corinthians 7:1b.

We are told to cleanse ourselves at the root—which
resides in our soul—as well as in our spirit (2 Corinthians
7:1). To ignore our soul (or flesh) will only perpetuate its fruit.
Our spirit will become contaminated if our soul rules over it.

In announcing the Lamb of God who takes away the
sin of the world, John the Baptist said, "...the axe is laid to
the root of the trees..." (Luke 3:9). Thus, we must kill more
than just our superficial natures, if we are to bear godly
fruit. We must examine and deal with the motives of our
hearts. Furthermore, to be involved in individual, corporate,
and national repentance, the deep roots in our soul must
first be severed.

Facing Yourself Honestly

When a Jezebel spirit becomes entwined with a
human soul, the roots of the demonic spirit must be discerned. This understanding comes from the Holy Spirit who
awakens our spirit to His lack of rule in our lives. He does
this by conviction, not condemnation.

God must reveal the point of weakness at which a
demonic spirit has access into a person's life. In closing this
door, a person will eliminate the threat of that demonic
spirit returning. Any lingering threats that may try to
reopen this door must also be dealt with. Therefore, a continuing spiritual vigil must be maintained until complete
healing has taken place (2 Corinthians 13:5).

Under great stress, a person who has seemingly been freed from a Jezebel spirit may fall back temporarily into former patterns of manipulation and control. Although they may have repented and been delivered of this spirit, their weak or wounded areas may not have had sufficient time to heal. Old habits may resurface. For this reason, if leadership does not pay attention, the individual may again become a problem.

OUT OF CONTROL BEHAVIOR

If an individual's problems came as a result of a dominant father or mother, an individual may need to ask themselves with whom he or she vies for control. They may still be in bondage to a controlling mother. They may have married a strong mate with whom they compete for control. If the threat of losing control is merely perceived, such as having a general fear of authority, they may overreact by challenging any authority figure for control. Whichever is the case, sound spiritual reasoning *must* be made in order for the individual to trust that others will not dominate, bruise or belittle them in the future.

Such an individual will readily sense an accusing, critical, or judgmental attitude towards them. This will quickly shut the door to any ministry of restoration. To minister deliverance will require great compassion. Remember, ministry succeeds when God initiates it and when His skill and wisdom are present.

CHANGE IS A PROCESS

Once an individual is freed from this demonic spirit, their spirit must be healed and strengthened. The entire process will take time. The person must be given time to mature spiritually. Leadership would be premature and should *not* be placed on this individual until deliverance, healing, and restoration is complete. A new foundation will need to be laid in the person's life. This may be difficult for a pastor to do. Especially if the pastor is timid, fearful, or angry at what the individual has done.

It is not unusual for the person who has operated with a Jezebel spirit to have a true prophetic call from God. This gift has simply been perverted, distorted, and misused. Redemption, healing, and maturity can be a wonderful gift that destroys the work of the evil one. Perhaps this is why Satan desires to pervert the gift—so it will not damage his own empire.

Pastors should take caution if they try to lightly heal this wound. Handling the situation poorly—by granting mercy where a firm stand should be taken or by overreacting to the person—may cause the wound to deepen and result in irreversible damage to the individual. If the person's gift is reactivated too quickly, it will bury the person under the weight of adulation.

CONFESSING YOUR SINS TO GOD

No matter what spirit oppresses a person, each person *must* refuse to defend themselves and justify their behavior. They must search their heart and repent, turning away from sin. They must confess their sins to the Lord who promises to forgive and purify (1 John 1:9). Repentance is vital to the restoration process (2 Corinthians 7:10). Until full repentance comes, God cannot truly bless and heal us (Isaiah 59:20).

In asking for help, leaders need to demonstrate mercy and compassion to the wounded individual.

Remember, it is God's kindness that leads us to repentance (Romans 2:4). The writer of Hebrews warns us to encourage each other daily so that we are not hardened by sin's deceitfulness (Hebrews 3:12-13). We must avoid doing things that cause the person to refuse the healing process, and thereby fall further away from God (Matthew 18:7).

Pastors, leadership, and church members should be careful to not demonstrate an arrogant or hostile posture toward the individual seeking to be healed. Any attempt to control a wounded individual may drive them further into rebellion.

Restoration will take time. Even with Jezebel, God gave her time to repent (Revelation 2:21).

A FORERUNNER PROPHETIC SPIRIT

Centuries ago God sent His messenger, the prophet Elijah. He confronted Jezebel and her false prophets who were leading God's people astray. Now in these last days, God is releasing a prophetic message across the Earth. He is raising up men, women, and children who will be empowered and anointed with the spirit of Elijah. They will confront the spirit of Jezebel (Malachi 4:5-6).

As a forerunner spirit, the spirit of Elijah will once again "make ready a people prepared for the Lord" (Luke 1:17b). As we make ready for His coming, we need to lay the axe at the root of our fleshly natures (Matthew 3:10) and bear fruit worthy of the Lord.

Chapter 8

THE POINT OF NO RETURN

KENNETH, WHO PASTORED A large church of several thousand members, was experiencing an unusual number of problems. Indecision plagued his leadership, unity among church members began to unravel, and the church came under extreme financial hardship. A spirit of sickness and infirmity began to powerfully assault the intercessors and their families. It was the first time that such an intense and unrelenting attack had come against the church. Even Kenneth's wife, who was normally healthy, became very ill.

In the midst of these calamities, a "savior" appeared—a woman stepped forward to run the daily prayer meetings. At first, Kenneth viewed the woman as an answer from God despite the fact that two intercessory leaders warned him about this woman. These intercessors claimed to have been given dreams and words of knowledge about this woman, which were hard for Kenneth to believe.

Then, a church member led by the Holy Spirit, happened to go to the new prayer leader's house. As she approached the door, she was startled by strange noises coming from inside. Concerned, she peeked in the front window. She was horrified to find the woman kneeling on the floor, chanting, and sticking pins in dolls that were dressed like Kenneth's wife and other various church leaders. Later, it was discovered that the woman was praying for the death of Kenneth's wife so that she could become his next wife. Sadly, the woman was deceived into thinking that her actions were for the ultimate good of the church. She truly believed Kenneth's wife was holding the church back.

PROGRESSIVE DEVELOPMENT

Left unchecked, a Jezebel spirit will drive a person deeper into occult development. This spirit will seek to destroy the pastor's home and the life of a church. Unfortunately, this ravaging pattern of events has been replayed countless times by "the mistress of sorceries, who sells ... families" (Nahum 3:4).

Not every individual in your church who operates in a Jezebel spirit will run the full range of activities listed in this book. More than likely, you will find believers in your church family who are innocently deceived by these demonic forces. Since they do *not* understand God's Word, they will be unable to rightly discern the spirits that drive them (1 John 4:1; Romans 1:22). Pastors will need to lovingly, but firmly, confront these individuals. If they do not, the person under the influence of that spirit will be carried further into greater evil—not to mention the residual effect that will be left in the church for years to come as the following story illustrates.

A RESIDENTIAL SPIRIT

Glenn attended a spiritually vibrant church. He had an unusual ability to garner sympathy from others. For years, his wife had been sick and Glenn had been constantly fighting various illnesses. However, one never really knew if this sickness was real or psychosomatic.

Glenn seemed to focus his pleas on the wealthy members of the church. Out of sympathy, many funneled money to him. Since Glenn was a beloved, grandfatherly figure, many began to believe that Glenn could do no wrong. Even the pastors and elders felt sorry for Glenn. Although they recognized his manipulation, they tolerated it and showed displaced mercy. As a result, a spirit of self-pity and pseudo-spirituality began to spread like a cancer through the Body.

While this charismatic church embraced the gifts of the Holy Spirit, they became impotent to do the works of the Kingdom. The Jezebel spirit that drove Glenn now became resident within the church. Furthermore, this spirit was seen as a form of godliness. Over time, pastors came and went, battling this unseen, spiritual force. Although the church had been given many prophetic words, God's promises never came to pass under the weight of this dark spirit. The Jezebel spirit became a part of the DNA of the church. Even though Glenn was later confronted by a pastor, and thereby left the church, taking several families with him, this demonic spirit still remained. The spiritual lethargy permeated the air and a cloak of death filled the atmosphere.

Although a Jezebel spirit likes to attach itself to a person, it can infiltrate and permeate the atmosphere of an entire congregation. Then, it will curtail, detour, or even kill prophetic words of invitation to a higher calling for that Body of believers. Consequently, a lack of confrontation due to unsanctified mercy can influence the spiritual impact of even a mature church. Remember, all unchecked sin will eventually ripen and bring forth fruit that leads to death.

THOSE WHO ARE NOT CHRISTIANS

Today, many well-meaning believers who operate in a Jezebel spirit may simply need revelation concerning their error. Most likely, this spirit has not fully matured in their life. Other individuals may resemble the mature Jezebel spirit portrayed in Scripture. Usually these individuals do not know the Lord. They have deliberately joined with a church to destroy it through occult means.

As I have mentioned earlier, we see a clear example of this diabolical scheme in Acts 16. A slave girl who was possessed with a spirit of divination met Paul and Silas on their way to a prayer meeting. Being drawn by their anointing, she began following them announcing, "These men are the servants of the Most High God, who proclaim to us the way of salvation" (Acts 16:17).

The devilish strategy was this: in associating with the apostles, the slave girl would appear to have been "endorsed" by Paul and Silas. Thus, when they continued on their missionary journey, the slave girl would have been positioned to step into their place. Thereby, Satan would be able to pervert the gifts and callings that Paul had conferred upon the church in Macedonia. By way of deception, the enemy could turn their hearts toward another god, Satan.

BALAAM'S ERROR

Balaam, the soothsayer (Joshua 13:22), also drew upon the occult for revelation and empowerment. In Hebrew, the word "soothsayer" is *quacam,* which means to determine by magical scroll. In using the word soothsayer, Scripture suggests that Balaam perverted his prophetic anointing by practicing the magical arts. We must understand that in the beginning, God spoke to Balaam. However, it was Balaam who chose to follow darkness, which led to his own demise.

Balak, King of Moab, sent messengers to ask the prophet Balaam to curse Israel. He offered Balaam a hefty reward. However, Balaam was forbidden by God to prophesy against Israel. Hoping God would change His mind, Balaam questioned God. Demonstrating his unbroken will through defiance and insubordination, Balaam became increasingly controlling. In this way, he was like Jezebel. He practiced manipulation and control until he passed the point of no return. With stubborn rebellion and manipulative control, Balaam's life mirrors the progression of a Jezebel spirit.

ULTERIOR MOTIVES

A subtle distinction exists between entreating God as an intercessor and seeking to override God's commands as a manipulator. A person's motive distinguishes the two because it will discern personal gain from corporate gain. Since God is able to search our hearts and discern our motives, He knew that Balaam wanted to manipulate Him in order to claim the reward. Consequently, Balaam's motive was driven by selfish desires.

As an intercessor, Abraham entreated God for the salvation of Sodom and Gomorrah (Genesis 18). Moses, whom God said was the most humble man on the face of the Earth, interceded on behalf of the Hebrew children. Moses asked God to take his life rather than wipe out his country-men (Exodus 32:32). God heard the cries of both Abraham and Moses and intervened. As such, intercession seeks restoration and building up of the things of God. Jezebel, on the other hand, seeks to unravel and destroy the things of God.

God may choose to deny a prayer request for His own reasons. When this happens, how we respond to God's refusal will determine everything.

INSUBORDINATION

Wrong responses lie in an attitude of subtle question-ing and cajoling. These arise from a heart of insubordination. Just as rebellion is as witchcraft, the Lord says that insubor-dination is as idolatry (1 Samuel 15:23). In the Hebrew, insubordination means "to push, to press, to urge." A heart of insubordination refuses to be persuaded by those in authori-ty. This individual will distrust, resist, and look for a way to thwart authority. They will do anything to get what they want.

As Scripture reveals, God played along with Balaam's insubordination (Numbers 22:20). But once God plays along with our game, beware! His judgment is waiting on the threshold.

DISTINCTIONS

Although a child will question, urge, and insist on his or her way, this does *not* mean the child has a Jezebel spirit. However, it does indicate that the child is developing a strong will which will need to be corrected. The same is true with a Christian who has an insistent, strong will. Ultimately, this individual will needs to be yielded and submitted to the Lord as well as the spiritual authorities placed over him or her.

DISCERNING MOTIVES

Whenever a motive to usurp authority is discerned, confrontation *must* come from the pastor. A pastor must personally question the individual and discern this person's motives. This requires that an individual will need to examine their own heart. In addition, this confrontation should be done with great gentleness (Galatians 6:1), seeking to avoid putting the person in a defensive posture.

However, be prepared. A person with a Jezebel spirit will try to convince a pastor or leadership that they are innocent, denying any wrong doing or underhandedness. They will insist their insights and methods are correct. Furthermore, these appeals will usually have a controlling, demanding spirit behind them.

GIVING IMPURELY

When Balaam's questioning did not accomplish his goals, he tried another tactic. He offered a sacrifice to God, hoping God would relent and grant his request (Numbers 23:1-3). Balaam's sacrifice, however, was an attempt to manipulate God. In a similar way, carnally minded individuals may give a gift or a sacrifice to procure God's favor.

When Balaam tried to entice God, it suggested that his heart was hardened and insensitive toward the Lord. Balaam believed that he could wheedle God. He had applied that logic to other gods—evil spirits who had given him knowledge by occult means. Now he was unable to distinguish Jehovah God from other gods. Naturally, Balaam's enticement failed.

A similar fate awaits someone operating with a Jezebel spirit. They will sacrifice much, mostly in the eyesight of others. They will dance, cry, raise their hands, fast, and go on various spiritual campaigns in order to move the hand of God. But God's arm will not be twisted by their spiritual ploys. God will not move on behalf of any individual whose motives are impure.

If someone with a Jezebel spirit does this before God, more than likely they will do it before the pastor. Like Balaam, they will bait, entice, and sell themselves to obtain power and endorsement. This individual *must* be confronted during these campaigns and shown their need for repentance.

INTENT TO INJURE

Look, these women caused the children of Israel, through the counsel of Balaam, to trespass against the Lord in the incident of Peor, and there was a plague among the congregation of the Lord—Numbers 31:16.

Balaam's next ploy was manipulation that proved costly to others. Manipulation, in itself, is wrong. Coupled with malice, it becomes evil. When malice is evident, confrontation must occur. According to Webster's Dictionary, to manipulate means "to manage or control artfully or by shrewd use of influence, especially in an unfair or fraudulent way." Manipulation involves skill and influence. It is often used underhandedly or covertly, in order to gain an advantage.

Prostituting his prophetic gift by the practice of divination for hire, Balaam manipulated the men of Israel with intent to harm. He exploited their weakness by placing beautiful women before them and causing them to stumble sexually. Thereby, the Jews also forsook their love of Jehovah God and committed spiritual adultery. Having calculated their downfall, Balaam knew their sin would force God to judge them. Thus, it had the same effect as Balaam demanding God curse Israel. Hence, Balaam would acquire his reward and Israel would be cursed.

Balaam's heart was hardened to the Lord (Numbers 22:7, 24:1). He was indifferent, cruel, and bitter. Sadly, in the end, Balaam was not known as a prophet of God, but as a soothsayer.

MANIPULATION GRIEVES THE HOLY SPIRIT

On one hand, most of us can recognize the evil in manipulating others with malice. But someone with a Jezebel spirit may justify their evil actions by the supposed good it will eventually bring. The outcome makes no difference—an individual is deceived when he or she uses manipulation, even for the supposed welfare of others.

Unfortuately, many believe they are justified in their actions because "it's for the greater good" of the church. Their logic may sound spiritual, even unselfish, in their own distorted way of thinking. But do not be deceived. Manipulation comes from a wrong spirit. It does *not* reflect submission to God's authority and order. Even if this person is in leadership, manipulation by anyone grieves the Holy Spirit.

Although not all manipulation is malicious, it is *always* wrong because it involves setting up people or circumstances to gain a desired end result. It is self-serving, even when we think it's for the good of others. Manipulation actually promotes our thoughts above God's thoughts. Whenever we push our ideas ahead of waiting for God to act, we reveal our pride, which is a form of idolatry. Therefore, manipulation must be confronted in the Church and in personal relationships.

VEILED MANIPULATION

Rick had taken a pastoral position in a church that was known for its compassion to the poor. The church was struggling, and soon he realized why.

Rick discovered that the person who started most of the gossip sat outside his office. His secretary was revealing personal information about everyone who came for counseling, who gave gifts, or who had problems of any kind. After a series of unheeded warnings, Rick had to let her go. This was done properly, yet he began hearing rumors of how heartless he had been. Even his elders, who had initially agreed with him, later questioned every decision he made.

Soon, Rick discovered a second problem. His now former secretary was a very good friend of the church cleaning woman who had been attending the church for years. This woman would periodically come up with strange, prophetic-sounding dreams. Whenever the Holy Spirit would anoint a service, this woman took great delight in telling everyone that she had dreamed about it happening. Rick, however found it hard to keep track of all her dreams. Furthermore, he struggled to understand how she applied a dream to a particular event. To complicate matters, this woman was in her 60's and used her "prophecies," along with her ill health, to elicit sympathy from others. They, in turn, would feel sorry for her and give her money.

In time, this woman became the "real boss" of the church because she had manipulated leadership with her pseudo-spirituality. Whatever she said became the final word! She was also a worse gossiper than Rick's former secretary. Feigning humility, she claimed that she never knew why God would give her these revelations. But none of her prophecies were ever more than fragmentally true, at best.

The turning point came when Rick caught her prophesying about a situation she had discovered, by shuffling through papers left on his desk. On this occasion, Rick had forgotten to clear his desk, which was his usual practice. When she claimed to have received the revelation from God, that was the last straw. Rick let her go with a month's severance pay. However, she contacted each board member and leader claiming she was terminated because of her friendship with Rick's former secretary. In a surprising turn of events, the board and leadership insisted that Rick reinstate her. Within a year, Rick left the church and three years after that, the church died.

TWISTED THINKING

Today, many pastors have felt the effects of a fully developed and demonically empowered Jezebel spirit. Some have had curses placed on them through carnal prayers of well-meaning people, supposedly to accomplish "God's will." Individuals given to a Jezebel spirit have a conscience that has been seared—calling good "evil" and evil "good." Their speculations have become futile and their hearts have become darkened. Scripture says they are without excuse.

> Thinking themselves to be wise, they became fools—Romans 1:20-22.

When an individual given over to a Jezebel spirit reaches this stage of maliciousness, confrontation and removal must take place. The time for repentance has past.

VIOLENCE AND AGGRESSION

> And she wrote letters in Ahab's name, sealed them with his seal, and sent letters to the elders and the nobles who were dwelling in the city with Naboth. She wrote in the letters, saying 'Proclaim a fast, and seat Naboth with high honor among the people; and seat two men, scoundrels, before him, saying, 'You have blasphemed God and the king.' Then take him out, and stone him, that he may die—1 Kings 21:8-10.

In this account, Jezebel proclaimed a fast and planted false witnesses to achieve her objectives. Similarly, someone given over to a Jezebel spirit may use spiritual disciplines while stirring up accusations designed to support his or her cause. This may take the form of verbal malice or even overt forms of hostility. These attacks increase in intensity toward the intended victim, as demonic spirits empower Jezebel and its influence. Such actions illustrate deeply rooted animosity and hatred toward those who disagree with Jezebel's will and desires.

116

In the end, an individual fully given over to a Jezebel spirit maligns, disgraces another individual, and seeks to destroy a person's influence. They do this to speaking evil of their victim's spirituality and destroying the person's influence. Jezebel illustrated this when she took Naboth's vineyard. Scripture reveals not only the strength of her malice, but also the extent of her violence and aggression.

An individual given over to a Jezebel spirit may confine their actions to emotional, verbal, or mental abuse. They may explode with rage. While doing so, often this person justifies their actions by continuing to believe the end justifies the means.

MURDEROUS RAGE

Murder is an evil tool used to subjugate the will of another. Jezebel plotted to frame Naboth and then kill him—all in the proper religious form of the day—since he refused to sell his vineyard to Ahab who coveted it. She coerced two false witnesses to accuse Naboth of cursing God before his leaders and his neighbors. Then she compelled the elders of Israel to comply with the Law and stone him. Although she was "religious," she was guilty of murder.

In essence, Jezebel's greatest act of control was murder—whether it was Naboth or the hundreds of God's prophets she had killed. Balaam also brought about the destruction of many. Both Balaam and Jezebel, however, were executed by a kingly figure. Balaam was slain at the command of Moses, and Jezebel was killed at the command of Jehu.

So it must be with the Church today. A pastor must not allow innocent people to be injured or destroyed by someone's lust for power and control. An individual with a

Jezebel spirit who operates maliciously cannot be tolerated. Pastoral leadership *must* remove this dark influence in their church. This principle is exactly what the apostle Paul ordered the Church in Corinth to do, when he admonished them to cast out the young man who was sexually involved with his stepmother (1 Corinthians 5).

PRACTICED SKILLS

An individual with a Jezebel spirit is skilled in getting their way. They may use tactics of flattery, persuasion, sexual seduction, slander, lying, accusation, intimidation, secrecy, persecution, framing another person for a wrong done, as well as generating emotional or spiritual dependency in someone. These individuals are driven by jealousy, rivalry, elitism, and a need to self-promote, dominate, and monopolize someone's time and attention. Furthermore, these individuals will malign anyone who gets in their way.

When left unchecked, this spirit will cause someone to actively pursue one leader to the next, stating their case to gain acceptance. Like a rebellious child going from one parent to the other, a person with a Jezebel spirit searches out someone to agree with their grievances. They will seek to influence others to heed their selfish demands. If a situation is not resolved to their satisfaction, Jezebel will malign–insinuate, badmouth, smear–their target and plant unnecessary doubts in the minds of others. They will also coyly violate disciplinary instructions, in an attempt to garner misguided sympathy and support. This tactic seems to soothe Jezebel's sense of injustice.

JEALOUSY

A spirit of jealousy plays a key role in fueling a Jezebel spirit. Jealousy seeks to monopolize the attention, admiration, or energy of its subjects. When coupled with control, a person driven by jealousy will seek to eliminate any competition. Jezebel will be threatened in a unique way by gifted prophetic people, because through revelation Jezebel's cloaked schemes are revealed. A prophetic intercessor whose prayer can depose a Jezebel spirit's powerbase is likewise a formidable foe. Thus, a Jezebel spirit despises authentic intercessory prayer and anointed prophetic ministries. True prophetic anointing manifests a God-ordained spiritual authority. Jezebel, who seeks to control others, will be frustrated by godly authority and threatened by those to whom it is entrusted.

ACCUSATION

Accusation is another common tool used by an individual with a Jezebel spirit. When this spirit is fully developed, demons assist the person to intimidate and induce fear in others. Accusation's power is satanic. It sows fear in an individual's heart. It causes people to run. Satan is the accuser of the brethren (Revelation 12:10), as well as the father of lies. A spirit of accusation has no truthful rationale behind it. Therefore, it cannot be reasoned with. It can only be dealt with as the Holy Spirit enlightens those in leadership to the issues. As with Korah, there will always be a tassel to camouflage the real issue—a spirit of lawlessness.

Those who walk in an accusing spirit are actually agreeing with the doctrine of demons. Therefore, God will hold them accountable, no matter what situation they are trying to correct. This is why the apostle James says that wherever you find slander and accusation, there also exists every evil thing (James 3:16).

An accusing spirit also works hand-and-glove with a religious spirit. Together, they will be a formidable and unrighteous force at work in a church, forging a critical base of support for Satan's cause.

Pastors and leaders who seek to deal with a Jezebel spirit should be aware of operating in an accusing spirit. If a pastor or leader brings a charge against Jezebel, it must be based on factual evidence supported by witnesses. Accusations, on the other hand, are based on supposition— what you believe is going on. Accusations are fueled by fear and will only result in denial and a "kickback" of charges in retaliation against a pastor, causing a pastor to lose favor with leadership.

Chapter 9

THE HEART
OF THE MATTER

B Y ALL APPEARANCES, BRENDA and Brad were a successful young couple. They dressed impeccably, were athletic, and drove BMWs. After becoming Christians, they channeled their ambitious drive for success into becoming deeply involved in church. They became active in various church ministries, holding dinners and prayer meetings. Their winsome and outgoing personalities attracted many. It seemed they were born for ministry.

Brenda and Brad gained the attention of Henry, the senior pastor. Their bond of friendship grew. Soon, Brad became Henry's associate pastor. But trouble was brewing just under the surface. On the outside, Brenda and Brad seemed to have the perfect marriage. Brad was poised and strong, but with his new position, Brenda was slowly becoming more intimidating. She could be emotionally overwhelming. After four years on staff, the pastor began to notice that her opinions now seemed to overrule Brad's wishes. He would simply cave into Brenda's strong and unflinching will.

Just as she had done with Brad, Brenda began to exert her strong will toward Henry. If she was not given a position for which she had lobbied, Brenda would pout and vent her disappointment at being overlooked. This unchecked rebellion was now turning into anger and bitterness. Although she maintained a face of compliance in front of Henry, she began to spread lies, saying he had a deep-seeded hatred of women. Although she had never approached Henry about her feelings, he had begun to hear rumors of what was being said behind his back.

On several occasions, Henry approached Brad about the rumors. This strategy seemed to quiet Brenda, but the calm was only momentary. Periodically, Brenda's anger would explode in staff meetings. During those times, she would confront Henry in a hostile and derogatory way. Soon, Brenda was meeting privately with other leader's wives and stirring up dissention. Two staff members resigned as a result.

From behind the scenes, Brenda had hoped to stage a coup and instate Brad as the senior pastor. She believed he would make a much better pastor than Henry. However before this could happen, the people began to scatter and run. Half the church left. Then, just when Brenda sensed the ruse was up and Henry was aware that she was the real problem, she convinced Brad to resign. However, Brad never realized what his wife had done.

GESTATION TIME

As seen in this story, a Jezebel spirit matures over time. This developmental process involves an individual gradually accepting demonically inspired thoughts. Over time, these thoughts become justified in their mind and lead them to take action which they believed was from God.

As this spirit matures, it will bring forth an abundance of prickly, poisonous, and deadly fruit, which is often disguised as enticing and spiritual. Those who reach for this fruit are pricked by hidden thorns, causing them to bleed, and are poisoned once they eat of its fruit.

COUNTERFEIT VOICES

The Jezebel spirit is a treacherous impostor within the Church. It counterfeits the true prophetic gift and it imitates and maligns the proper function of prophetic ministries. Other darker counterfeits to the prophetic—psychics, clairvoyants, palm-readers who practice witchcraft, divination, and sorcery—have arisen in recent years to speak about the supernatural. It may surprise you to learn that a Jezebel spirit is even more deceptive than these, simply because it is less obvious to the untrained eye.

Although an individual given over to a Jezebel spirit may not practice the black arts or the deep secrets of Satan, they share the same clandestine, demonic roots with those in the occult. In fact, individuals controlled by a Jezebel spirit often bear greater fruit, because its actions are more covert and its roots become more entrenched before becoming noticed.

Every church that embraces a prophetic ministry will have to contend with the Jezebel spirit because it mimics the prophetic gifts and callings of God. This spirit comes to destroy the prophetic gift. Consequently, since it works covertly, its activities are extremely treacherous.

An individual given over to this spirit often tries to enhance and strengthen their powerbase by attracting and controlling others, acting much like a spiritual magnet. Pastors and leaders will need to recognize the working of this covert spirit because it will seek to divide groups and stir up contention, confusion, and deception in the Church.

NECESSARY DISTINCTIONS

A clear distinction must be made between an immature prophetic person and someone who has a Jezebel spirit. Those who are prophetically immature are merely trying to find their rightful place in the Body. They may lack wisdom and humility, however their intention is *not* to destroy the church. Overly eager and immature prophetic individuals will do things that seem foolish or unwise. But just as we don't kill our children for their immaturity, neither should we kill those who are in prophetic infancy. Pastors and leaders must make allowances for a young prophetic individual's childishness. They must overcome their weariness of having young prophets who need to be trained.

As we—in the wisdom and counsel of the Lord—sharpen and hone the skills of those with prophetic gifts, it will bring forth valor and purity in the prophetic ministry. Eventually, such individuals will bring insight, revelation, and wisdom to the Body of Christ. Thus, all the petty difficulties of this gestation period will seem worth the time and effort expended.

During this developmental season, it's especially important to *not* maim or abort the gifts of a young prophetic person by accusing them of having a Jezebel spirit. Pastors and leaders must learn to discern how to bring correction and how to nurture a budding prophetic gift, without wounding or killing this person's spirit.

Sometimes the difference between an immature prophetic person and someone who operates with an immature Jezebel spirit is very subtle. To discern the difference involves looking at the heart of the matter. A young prophetic person begins with a heart to serve God.

Although someone operating with a Jezebel spirit may have started out with a heart to serve God, at some point they have departed from that path into one of self-promotion. Several additional points of departure are described more fully below.

1. SELFISH AMBITION

As Scripture advises us:

> Let nothing be done through selfish ambition
> or conceit, but in lowliness of mind let each of
> you esteem others better than himself—
> Philippians 2:3.

Loving the acclaim of others, an individual with a Jezebel spirit will often give themself a title or seek after a leadership position. Being elitist, they will regard a certain position as being "the most anointed" and dismiss another as being "less anointed" or as not having a voice in the church or in spiritual matters.

They will become zealous to market their gifts and broaden their sphere of influence. Often such individuals will not consult the Lord about where and when to minister. They will simply yield to the need for greater press. As their success increases, they will run to deliver many words, although God has not sent them. They may even believe that as their reputation increases, God's Kingdom will also increase. However, they are sadly deceived.

On the other hand, young prophetic individuals may gravitate initially toward the distinction thrust on them. But as they mature, most will shun any fanfare or publicity. They will realize that being in the limelight only serves to blind their eyes to God's high calling and that fame actually detracts from spending time alone with the Lord.

Individuals who are called to prophetic ministry must also desire to be held accountable for their words and actions. They should welcome others pointing out their errors and weaknesses. They must learn to submit to spiritual authority. In the process of submission, we learn to die to our self-will. This is an incredibly painful process, but all of us must pay the price and crucify our soul, as well as our fleshly desires. Willingness to submit every aspect of our life and ministry to the Lord must be evident in those who stand to lead His Church. One of the hallmarks of someone with the heart of God is how they respond to correction. Jezebel chaffs when corrected, but a spiritual person will repent.

2. PERSONAL GAIN

While a prophetic person goes through a costly breaking process (Nehemiah 5:14-19), an individual with a Jezebel spirit rarely makes such sacrifices. For the most part, Jezebel will express a persistent drive to demonstrate their "prophetic insight." In doing so, they have an ulterior motive and will insist upon some sort of payback— recognition, fame, money, clothing, or various privileges lavished upon them by individuals easily infatuated with supernatural insight.

Quickly, this self-centered individual will notice their prophetic insight can open doors. Consequently, they will give into the temptation to use their gift, mixed with human prognostication and personal opinion. Such individuals may read people's souls and later present this soulish insight as divinely inspired prophecy.

When this tainted revelation comes forth, it will lead astray those who are not in tune with the Holy Spirit. Once again, the Jezebel spirit seeks to tear apart while the prophetic ministry seeks to serve and encourage others. Even if a prophetic word is a difficult one, it should leave the hearer with hope, not condemnation.

3. A LUST FOR LIFE

Sensual appetites will often run rampant in an individual who operates with a Jezebel spirit. A spirit of lust will eat away at their soul, until it gains control of them.

Such lust is not simply sexually oriented. Money, favor, or recognition may feed their ambition and offer desired results. An insatiable thirst for self-indulgent pleasures will grow. Conversely, the work of the Cross will cease to be manifested in this person's life.

4. DEMONIC ENTANGLEMENT

As an individual approaches an intermediate level of demonic entanglement, their purposes will become more cunning and deliberate. The individual will try to control the actions of friends, families, and churches. Whenever false humility, lies, and flattery do not bring about the expected esteem and recognition, this individual often resorts to anger, condemnation, accusation, and domination. This individual will become increasingly more problematic. At this stage, they will have become quite skilled and able to rationalize their brusque behavior with confusing spiritual language. Anyone who attempts to confront them without being prepared will walk away scratching their heads in confusion and will dismiss the thought the person had Jezebellic tendencies—even though their initial discernment was correct.

If this person's strong will and insubordination are not dealt with, they will rebel against any authority that does not agree with them. In addition, they will counsel others to rebel against pastoral authority—often presenting those who disagree with them as being spiritually blind or naive. This unchecked rebellion will open the door for other evil spirits to infiltrate them, their followers or even an entire church. Consequently, a sudden, violent verbal attack may arise and be specifically targeted toward individuals who do not show loyalty or submission to Jezebel. Meanwhile, church members who seem indifferent or complacent to this rebellion will end up serving as pawns in a demonic game of win or lose. Tragically, the end result will usually be a church split.

5. A SPIRIT OF LAWLESSNESS

The spirit of lawlessness is rampant in our culture today. Lawlessness is a term used to describe people who are not restrained or controlled by the law, especially God's Word. In essence, all rebellion against God is lawlessness (1 John 3:4). Those who were responsible for the death of

Jesus are characterized as lawless (Acts 2:23). The leader of the end-time rebellion, the Antichrist, is called the man of lawlessness (2 Thessalonians 2).

The spirit of lawlessness unleashes its attack on the Kingdom of God and drives individuals to rebel and oppose God's appointed leaders. This spirit inspires innuendoes, rumors, lies, slander, manipulation, and control by creating schisms—or threatening to do so. Thus, when we covertly challenge and slander godly pastors and other ministries, we have violated God's established rules for His Kingdom. Such thinking is rebellion or sin.

> Whoever commits sin also commits *lawless-ness*, and sin is *lawlessness*—1 John 3:4.

Our omniscient God has foreknowledge of each pastor's theology, gifts, experiences, and personality. With infinite insight, God knows exactly how a pastor will carry out his or her ideas and plans for a church. Their strengths will probably be evidenced first, followed by their weaknesses—neither of which surprise God. Thus, a pastor known to hurt people in relationships, whether knowingly or unknowingly, is allowed to lead a church in spite of his or her weaknesses. God is patient, watching faithful pastors mature in character and gifting. If your pastor offends you, could it be God is using him or her to reveal your heart?

PROPER PROTOCOL

By speaking against God's established leaders, you are sowing seeds for your own destruction. Remember, Scripture tells us:

> Do not receive an accusation against an elder
> except from two or three witnesses—
> 1 Timothy 5:19.

The passage in Matthew 18 provides us with a proper protocol to follow with any church member, including a pastor or a leader who has sinned or is in error.

> Moreover if your brother sins against you, go
> and tell him his fault between you and him
> alone. If he hears you, you have gained your
> brother. But if he will not hear, take with you
> one or two more, that 'by the mouth of two or
> three witnesses every word may be estab-
> lished.' And if he refuses to hear them, tell it
> to the church. But if he refuses even to hear
> the church, let him be to you like a heathen
> and a tax collector—Matthew 18:15-18.

Even if your pastor is angry and controlling like Saul, you must demonstrate a heart of David. You must refrain from taking the opportunity to "kill" God's leader (1 Samuel 24). David waited for God to intervene and deal with Saul. May it never be said of you, as it was of Absalom, that you stole the hearts of the people away from your pastor (2 Samuel 15:4-6).

Let God judge your pastor. If you judge him or her, God will be justified in saying, "Since men have taken action, I will step back." Thus, God will allow us to live with the results of our actions. In addition, by taking judgement into our own hands, we then give the demonic arena a legal right to judge, hassle, harass, and come against us, simply because we have acted presumptively and have stepped out from under our covering. Therefore, it would be better to leave a church quietly, than to speak against God's anointed.

Some people erroneously think that because their gifts continue to be used, their actions are sanctioned by God. Remember what the Lord said:

> Not everyone who says to Me, 'Lord, Lord,' shall enter the kingdom of heaven, but he who does the will of My Father in heaven. Many will say to Me in that day, 'Lord, Lord, have we not prophesied in Your name, cast out demons in Your name, and done many wonders in Your name? And then I will declare to them, 'I never knew you; depart from Me, you who practice *lawlessness*!— Matthew 7:21-23.

Some of us may think that because we are casting out demons, healing the sick, raising the dead, or prophesying accurately that it indicates God's stamp of approval.

We may think we are within the will of God when we criticize our pastor, but God calls it lawlessness. As Jesus once said, "These people draw near to Me with their mouth, and honor Me with their lips, but their heart is far from Me" (Matthew 15:8). A heart dedicated and consecrated to the Lord honors the spiritual authority that God has established. A heart that rejects that authority allows lawlessness to influence their perceptions and decisions.

Please understand that I am not saying we cannot question a spiritual leader who has authority over us. Inquiry is an important process of maturity. However, what we do after a disagreement is critical. If our conversation becomes covert, hidden, and malicious, we are treading in the realm of lawlessness. Our actions depict lawlessness, especially if our intent is to remove that leader by the actions we take.

The early Church fathers felt there were only four reasons that warranted removing a pastor: moral failure; financial impropriety; teaching heresy; rage or uncontrolled emotions.

THE MYSTERY OF DECEPTION

For the *mystery of lawlessness* is already at work; only He who now restrains will do so until He is taken out of the way—
2 Thessalonians 2:7.

The word *mystery* is defined by Webster as "a religious truth that one can know only by revelation." Thus, the mystery of lawlessness will involve the condition of being deceived. When individuals are involved in lawless acts, they are often unaware of being in rebellion. They are misled by a mental stronghold of self-righteous thinking and are fooled into thinking they are doing God—and the church—a favor. Thus, they have elevated their way of thinking and are trying to correct someone God has chosen as their authority. Their actions demonstrate that they actually despise authority.

The mystery of lawlessness has been and is still powerfully at work in our culture. Furthermore, Satan has subtly persuaded many to embrace the concept of relativism that views ethical truths as being defined by individuals, groups, circumstances, and situations. Today, many believe there are no universal absolutes. Each person defines their own rules. Many believe that "what's right for one person is not right for another." Thus, tolerance becomes a cultural buzzword that disarms anyone who embraces biblical absolutes.

People who are deceived by lawlessness want to throw away all restraints and controls. They do not understand, however, that by rejecting God's laws we are led into greater licentiousness and enslavement to sin. When we practice lawlessness, it becomes easier to do it again. Thus, lawlessness leads to more lawlessness.

> I speak in human terms because of the weakness of your flesh. For just as you presented your members as slaves of uncleanness, and of *lawlessness* leading to more *lawlessness*, so now present your members as slaves of righteousness for holiness—Romans 6:19.

Historically, I have found that many who try to remove a pastor in one church will repeat their actions in another church. Thus, they develop a history of causing church problems. It's also true that churches launched from a church split often end up splitting themselves. In these situations, the spirit of Jezebel flourishes.

In Scripture, the spirit of lawlessness is linked to the spirit of lust or uncleanness. Together, these spirits corrupt the soul. Those who practice lawlessness walk according to their own ungodly lusts. They are called "sensual persons" by Jude (verse 19).

Lawlessness results in unfruitfulness and unanswered prayers. It causes us to ask amiss and for personal benefit (James 4:3). Lawlessness causes us to curse men that God has made. When we do that, we are inferring that God was unaware of whom He was making.

> With [the tongue] we bless our God...and with
> it we curse men, who have been made in the
> similitude of God—James 3:9.

Throughout Scripture, we are exhorted to *not* live according to this world, but to pursue peace with all men (Hebrews 12:14). It is also clear the relationship we should have with authority figures. We must treat them with respect (Romans 13:1-7). When we do, God will anoint us with the oil of gladness and we will have life forevermore (Psalm133).

God gives each of us the choice of becoming a vessel of honor or dishonor—to be mightily used of God or to be cast away from His presence (2 Timothy 2:20-21). Our willingness to choose obedience, even in the midst of disagreement, is key to walking as a vessel of honor.

> He who keeps His command will experience
> nothing harmful; and a wise man's heart dis-
> cerns both time and procedure, because for
> every matter there is a time and procedure,
> though the misery of man increases greatly—
> Ecclesiastes 8:5-6, NASB.

A CORRECT RESPONSE TO AUTHORITY

Since God has placed those in authority over us, we must be willing to submit to them. We should also make it a joy for them to watch over our souls.

> Obey those who rule over you, and be sub-
> missive, for they watch out for your souls, as
> those who must give an account. Let them do
> so with joy and not with grief, for that would
> be unprofitable for you—Hebrews 13:17-18.

Your willingness to submit to those in authority does not mean that you cannot have different ideas. You can experience great unity in the midst of great diverstiy. However, once a course of action has been taken by leadership, you need to support their decision. If you find yourself questioning the direction taken by leadership, then seek another church that is more in line with your ideals and calling. Furthermore, when making that change, do so with grace and humility, not with discord or strife. If you do not, Scripture says it will be "unprofitable."

> The king's heart is in the hand of the Lord,
> like the rivers of water; He turns it wherever
> He wishes—Proverbs 21:1.

As you examine your own heart, ask yourself: Do you really believe God can turn your pastor's heart? If so, then why not step back and pray? We serve a faithful and just God, who is capable of bringing about changes in the heart of your pastor. If God shares your beliefs and priorities for the church, you may witness the pastor responding to divine revelation, which affects a change in his or her decisions and actions. If God does not bring about the changes you desire, perhaps the more important issue is you, not your pastor! The question then becomes, "What is God trying to change in me?"

Accepting honest answers to questions such as these may point out areas in your life where God desires change. In this process, you may benefit from a deeper understanding of yourself. You will also grow closer to the Lord, as you look to Him to influence your pastor.

SOME BASIC ASSUMPTIONS

Before going further, you may want to consider the following presuppositions:

PREMISE 1: God is all knowing. God's knowledge is complete and extends to the past and the future.

PREMISE 2: God establishes all authority in its position.

PREMISE 3: God allowed decisions that placed your pastor in your church, knowing exactly what he or she would do.

PREMISE 4: God is *not* surprised by what your pastor is, or is not, doing.

PREMISE 5: God is all powerful and can cause your pastor to stop any course of action, should He choose. He could visit your pastor and tell him or her to stop, if God thought it was important to do so.

PREMISE 6: If God is not correcting your pastor, perhaps He is using the situation to work in your life, as well as in the life of your pastor.

PREMISE 7: If God is working in your life and in your pastor's life, then it would be wise to remember: Blessed are the merciful, for they shall receive mercy (Matthew 5:7). In showing mercy to your pastor, you will receive mercy from God.

PREMISE 8: To challenge pastoral authority, except for the four issues of moral failure, financial impropriety, teaching heresy, rage or uncontrolled emotions, is to act presumptively as if you are God. The consequences of such behavior may be grave.

Chapter 10

PREPARING TO MINISTER TO THE WOUNDED

I N THE SHORT SPAN of nearly two years, Joel watched his church shrink from 300 to 120 members. During that time, he noticed a particular woman who embodied what any pastor would have been thrilled to have in a church member—someone who seemed supportive, humble, prayerful, and sincere. One Saturday morning, however, his eyes were painfully opened. The woman, who was a divorcée, arrived at a couple's marriage retreat and forcibly tried to take over the microphone during one session. Joel could not figure out what had come over her.

A few weeks later, his reservations about the woman were fortified when he opened the mail and found a letter from this woman's friend. Worded as if God had dictated the letter, the writer said the divorcée was Joel's true spiritual mate and strongly insinuated that he should leave his wife, who was "holding him back spiritually." Since the divorcée did not actually write the letter, Joel was confused about how to confront this attack on his marriage.

One morning after a prayer meeting, he was having coffee with a small group that included the divorcée. She offered some "directions from God," and when he did not accept them, she became angry. In minutes her emotions escalated. She slammed her fist down on the table, spilling cups of coffee, and left.

A few weeks later, when a prophetic ministry came to the church for a conference, the prophet gave a word to the pastor. He warned about a so-called "spiritual mate" who was trying to rise up in the church. Surprised by the revelation, Joel spoke privately to the woman about this prophetic word. The following day in church, the divorcée stood and walked to the front, calmly and firmly interrupting the speaker. Cloaked in false humilty, she read a written and slanderous rebuke. By that time, the pastor had enough. He told the divorcée she was wrong in her assessment and he wanted to see her in his office the next day. But she never showed up. She left the church, but the damage had been done. Within a year, the church died.

PERSONAL ASSESSMENT

Confrontation of this spirit is not as easy as it may seem. Because of its many faces, this spirit is hard to diagnose. It can appear prayerfully submissive one minute and bold and brash the next. It may simply appear concerned for the well-being of the church. Like an octopus with eight spindly arms, this spirit is a nightmare to dislodge.

Before confronting someone with a Jezebel spirit, a pastor must first assess his or her own personal and spiritual condition. Danger lies in being tempted to react defensively and to misuse your power.

If a pastor feels intimidated by previous encounters with a Jezebel spirit, future scenarios may leave him or her feeling bitter, resentful, and angry. If these feelings exist, it simply signals that the pastor is not ready to effectively deal with this spirit.

Before going further, the pastor may need to appoint someone with wisdom, discernment and spiritual authority, as well as a "eunuch mentality." This may require that a pastor look for a specialist in deliverance ministry. There are a growing number of ministries that specialize in such concerns as this.

Anyone who is going to address the Jezebel spirit operating through a person must pause and assess their own spiritual condition. Are you feeling any jealousy, strife, envy, or malice toward an authority figure—past or present— in your own life? Do you harbor any hidden feelings of rejection or being overlooked? Such feelings may lead you to overreact to this spirit. Until these attitudes are overcome, addressing a spirit of insubordination and rebellion in another cannot be fully or powerfully accomplished. In addition, there are other issues to be dealt with.

FRUSTRATION AND ANGER

...you who are spiritual restore such a one in a spirit of gentleness, considering yourself lest you also be tempted—Galatians 6:1.

Frustration and anger mount when we do not deal with each issue immediately. No one likes to be controlled by another person. If a pastor has been wounded by someone with a Jezebel spirit, then he or she is an ideal candidate for mishandling a ministry situation. Scripture warns us:

For the wrath of man does not produce the righteousness of God—James 1:20.

Since an individual with a Jezebel spirit often uses criticism and accusation, such demonic spirits cannot be driven out by a pastor who reacts in like manner. A pastor must first confront and deal with his or her own critical and accusing spirit.

EVIL FOR EVIL

When control and manipulation are evidenced in a pastor's life, he or she will become defenseless against a Jezebel spirit. In counteracting manipulation with manipulation, the pastor will have failed to walk in the fruit of the Holy Spirit. Moreover, God does *not* honor our actions when we return evil for evil.

Whenever we retaliate this way, our anger has twice the impact. First, we lash out because we are angry with ourselves for allowing the wound to remain in our soul. Second, we react because we are angry with the person who manifests the same propensity toward sin. We are often guilty of attacking the very weaknesses in others that are evidenced in our lives.

When pastors feel insecure or uncertain of how to handle a situation, they may resort to intimidation. They do this to maintain control. Intimidation, however, will never bring true repentance or restoration, which should *always* be our goal. Intimidation will only produce a temporary remorse, feigned repentance, or withdrawal. Consequently, intimidation will abort any sincere opportunity to minister healing to a wounded person.

Attempting to create fear in someone else, by appearing more powerful, will only complicate the problem. It will drive a pastor to badger, belittle, and attempt to "back the person into a corner." Such methods will only birth more hostility. Or it will provoke the individual to stir up slander or plan acts of violence and rage.

When a pastor reacts to Jezebel in anger, Jezebel will begin to cower. These individuals will portray themselves as being a victim and you as being an ogre. This usually happens whenever others are present to witness your angry outburst, which will make it seems as if Jezebel is the underdog. If you haven't already experienced this, you will. It is only a matter of time.

DOMINEERING PASTORS

Instinctively, an individual with a Jezebel spirit will often mirror a pastor's manner of operation. If the pastor is self-promoting, the individual may feel the freedom to promote their gifts and abilities. If the leader is domineering, the individual may see this as having permission to always maintain the upper hand with others. If a domineering pastor should clash with a strong-willed Jezebel, then a fierce and ugly battle will arise.

I recommend that a pastor focus his or her attention on opposing the demonic stronghold in the person while demonstrating love toward the person. Any confrontation must be done in love to restore the person. Only a loving confrontation will compel an individual to experience brokenness. Jezebel will need to experience godly sorrow that leads to repentance.

If you face resistance by Jezebel, avoid the tendency to react scornfully. Remember, you are not wrestling against flesh and blood, but against the powers of darkness (Ephesians 6:12). Ask God to search your heart further. Then respond with great strength and determination to help the individual repent. If you are defensive or reactive, Jezebel may detect your insecurity. To disarm you, Jezebel may respond with a false mask of meekness.

Your confidence must be in the Lord. Believing that God has appointed you as shepherd over the flock will enable you to act valiantly and with compassion.

BITTERNESS TOWARD WOMEN

Memories of neglect from a mother, from prior romantic relationships, or from fluctuations in a marriage influence a pastor's ability to communicate and confront. Jezebel will usually sense a pastor's bitterness or areas of unresolved wounds. Therefore, a pastor must guard against transferring unsettled issues about a grandmother, mother, sister, or spouse to the individual operating under a Jezebel spirit.

Suspicion, strife, and vain imagination about potential conflicts will drive a pastor to eradicate anyone who seems unsubmissive. However, suspicion, strife, and vain imagination are spirits of witchcraft. If a pastor is tempted to operate in these ways, such spirits may have a foothold in him or her. A pastor will *not* be able to overcome Jezebel until freed of these heart issues. Furthermore, demonic spirits may attack a pastor or leader who arrogantly or smugly attacks a Jezebel spirit.

To operate in the wrong spirit is better described as operating in the power of the soul. Whenever we use our soul to conquer another's soul, we will fail to get God's needed counsel to gain the victory. Only by exercising the fruits of the Holy Spirit—love, joy, peace, longsuffering, kindness, goodness, faithfulness, gentleness, and self-control—can the power of the soul be conquered. Only a spiritual touch can produce eternal change in another.

Furthermore, trying to use the soul in this manner will bring disaster to a pastor, his or her family, and the church. A pastor must keep in mind that he or she is dealing with dark powers. This battle is not merely with a person. The enemy's success distorts our thinking and produces a spirit of fear, suspicion, or accusation in our hearts. Jezebel operates under the power of the soul. If you operate under the same power, you inflate the demonic spirit and it now controls both of you.

A TRAGIC ENCOUNTER

Shortly after his fortieth birthday, Martin was meeting with a couple from his church. He was convinced they had a Jezebel spirit. It was their second meeting and Martin had invited the elders. Although the first meeting had been volatile, Martin was prepared for this confrontation. The couple would not make him look bad, although they had threatened to do so.

Secretly, Martin hated confrontation. He avoided it. But he remembered two other occasions when he had failed to address this issue and the results had been devastating—two church splits. The last one cost Martin his position at a large prestigious church in another state. Martin made a resolve that he would never let such a thing happen again. He would snuff out any nonsense before it got worse. Tonight, the elders would witness this couple's hostile personal agenda just as he had in their previous meeting.

Two hours later, Martin sat with his face buried in his hands. He was deeply frustrated. Nothing had changed. No admission of guilt had been made by the couple. Furthermore, they showed no remorse for their actions. Instead, they acted coy and innocent. They even accused Martin of misunderstanding their words and actions.

During the meeting, the couple often said they were *only* trying to serve God. With tears running down their faces, they reminded Martin and the elders of all the times they had helped him and the church. Soft-spoken and seemingly humble, the couple questioned Martin's motives and claimed he was turning a molehill into a mountain.

With slight of hand, they had turned the tables on Martin. Listening to them, Martin even became confused and began to wonder if they were right. Perhaps his own fear and insecurity drove him to point his finger at them.

After the couple left, the elders further probed Martin about his accusations. They began to side with the couple. They also speculated about the reason for Martin's charges. Martin saw doubt creep into their faces. They were puzzled about his discernment and leadership skills.

Three months later, the couple stood up during the

church service and demanded Martin's resignation. They listed their reasons and worded their accusations as if God had spoken. When Martin refused to resign, they shouted, "Ichabod," meaning "the glory has departed from Israel". Then, they marched out of the church. Eighty church members filed out with them. Two months later, Martin took a sabbatical. Sadly, he never returned to the ministry again.

When Ministering to Others

You will need to encourage a person who has repented from using a Jezebel spirit to continue taking new steps forward. He or she must be encouraged to keep renewing his or her mind. They will need to recognize and adopt God's way of looking at things.

Activities that restore feelings of self-worth should be encouraged. Frequently, these individuals have a great desire to contribute in a worthwhile way. Servanthood, with healthy boundaries, is a key to restoration. However, their serving others should not be confused with them having authority. To give them authority at this time would be tantamount to giving an alcoholic a drink.

All areas of rebellion will need to be addressed. In an attitude of meekness, amends will need to be made in order to close the door to future inroads by the enemy.

Suggested Steps for Confrontation

Here are some suggestions for pastors who must confront an individual who operates with a Jezebel spirit:

1. Get counsel from others who are spiritually mature on any blind spots you have and how to handle the situation.

2. Pray before you speak in any confrontation. Ask the Holy Spirit to reveal hidden issues. It is amazing how issues will surface that had not been previously known, if you allow the Holy Spirit to do His work.

3. Ask the Holy Spirit for wisdom to help you discern what is spiritual, by discerning what demonic spirits they have embraced. Ask for discernment about what is natural or from the person's upbringing, such as harsh parental issues.

4. Always have someone in the room with you during any confrontation.

5. Confront each issue with grace, but also with firmness and candor. Be specific. You must explain the problems. Do not make the mistake of not revealing names and specific accusations.

6. At all costs, avoid becoming angry. Keep calm. Do not overreact or make the issue larger than it is.

7. Do not ignore the problem. It will *not* get smaller or disappear.

8. From the moment a problem is suspected, document all third-party information. Record dates, times, places, and what was said. Otherwise, trying to piece together tidbits of information will only lead to Jezebel's denial.

9. Get permission from third parties to use all testimonies, along with their names, in the meeting. If you do not, Jezebel will deny saying such things.

10. Tape record the meeting. Be sure to let the individual know that you are taping the meeting. Set the tape recorder in the open, for all to see.

If you follow these suggestions, be prepared for Jezebel to repent and apologize with great emotional passion. At the same time, do not be surprised when Jezebel, whom you thought had repented, recoils and strikes again with greater vengenance. If that happens, you need to repeat the above process of confrontation. If they will not hear you the second time, then you must remove them from the church.

RED FLAGS

Here are some early warning signs that pastors, in hindsight, have shared with me. Pastors may want to keep alert for these phrases that *could* indicate a storm brewing on the horizon.

1. "I just want to be your friend." More than likely, people who say these things will have expectations that you will never be able to meet.

2. "I just want to help you get to where God has called you." In other words, you cannot get to your destiny without them. Beware!

3. "There are no strings attached to my help. I just want to serve." However, you will find lots of hidden strings.

4. "You can trust me. I will always support you." They will support you as long as you do what they say!

5. "You do not acknowledge my gifting." In other words, they are asking you to give them more authority in the church.

6. "You do not understand me." This is a veiled cry for you to spend more time than you have available.

7. "You intimidate me. I do not feel like I can talk to you." In other words, they want their goals to become your goals.

147

8. "I have new revelation. The pastor has Old Testament understanding and I have New Testament understanding." In other words, they are right and you are wrong!

9. "The Lord has given me some things that I need to share with you." Duck! You'll probably be receiving a harsh spanking from them.

10. "My last pastor did not know how to use me or my gifts." In other words, "Let me have my way."

WORKING FOR OUR GOOD

If handled rightly, an attack by a Jezebel spirit will ultimately strengthen a church. God uses the fiery battles of life to train, strenthen, and refine us (1 Peter 4:12-19). As God once told me: Small battles produce small victories, but great battles produce great victories—in our lives, in our ministries, and in our churches.

Chapter 11

DISMANTLING JEZEBEL'S MANTLE

JEREMIAH WATCHED IN HORROR as Babylonian soldiers set fire to the Temple in Jerusalem. His eyes burned from the smoke as well as his own grief, as he watched buildings throughout the city become pillaged and set ablaze. He wondered why the people had not listened to him. Why had they allowed themselves to be influenced by the pagan nations around them? If *only* the Jews would have heeded the prophets! If only they would have listened to Moses!

Gazing at the billowing black pillar of smoke rise, Jeremiah stared as the flames consumed the Holy Place. Although they were God's chosen people, the Jews slowly became like the Babylonians. Now, they had fallen under God's judgment, just as Moses predicted.

But if you do not drive out the inhabitants of the land from before you, then it shall be that

149

those whom you let remain shall be irritants in your eyes and *thorns in your sides*, and they shall harass you in the land where you dwell. Moreover it shall be that I will do to you as I thought to do to them—Numbers 33:55-56, Italics mine.

A DEMONIC THORN

Any thorn will cause infection unless it is removed. A demonic thorn can prick the Church and cause infection, just as a splinter can inflame the skin and cause infection. The longer it is ignored, the greater the spread of infection. If neglected, the infection can spread and lead to amputation—or even worse, death.

To resolve the matter of a Jezebel spirit, God requires His servants to remove the demonic thorn that infects His Body. Godly confrontation is necessary in order for conviction and true repentance to occur.

Conviction and repentance occurs with the help of the Holy Spirit. Pastors cannot force repentance upon anyone because we are *not* the "convictor" of sin. The Holy Spirit has that responsibility. We can pray that the Holy Spirit will convict an individual who operates with a Jezebel spirit. However, if an individual's behavior becomes obviously malicious and damaging to others in the church, a pastor must confront the issue. Decisive and unified action is needed by the pastor and the eldership before God takes action, as He was about to do with Thyatira.

RESPONSIBILITY FOR REMOVAL

Responsibility for addressing a Jezebel spirit belongs to the pastor. As an overseer of the flock, a pastor has the authority to confront and remove any troublesome person or problem in a church.

A pastor should not expect a prophet to address this issue. A prophet's responsibility is only to reveal an individual who covertly operates in a Jezebel spirit. Remember, the prophet Elijah ran from Jezebel. His successor, Elisha, realized that only kings had the authority to remove Jezebel. Thereby, God instructed Elisha to anoint Jehu to be king.

APPROACHES TO CONSIDER

There are two basic approaches to take when confronting Jezebel. The first is to announce your conclusion (i.e., "you have a Jezebel spirit"), and then identify the reasons you drew that conclusion. This approach rarely works. The stigma of being called "Jezebel" is too offensive. Furthermore, the person has erroneously perceived that the Jezebel spirit is the Holy Spirit. Therefore, everything they have embraced becomes suspect. Since the Jezebel spirit counterfeits the Holy Spirit, they will have to admit that they were operating in the wrong spirit. They will need to acknowledge that the spirit which gave them comfort, power, insight, authority, value, and self-esteem is demonic. If they make such a confession, it will leave them feeling confused and disoriented, not knowing what to believe or who to trust.

For these reasons, I do not recommend taking this approach. More than likely, the person will not acknowledge their problem. They will continue to believe they heard from the Holy Spirit. Consequently, they will begin to mount a defensive campaign against you, trying to entrench themselves further in the church so that you cannot get rid of them. Or, they will leave the church. While this solves your immediate problem, the person remains unhealed. Pastors with a Kingdom mentality will grieve for the loss of God's original destiny for that person.

The second and more apostolic approach is to identify and address core issues before announcing your conclusion. In fact, you may never have to identify that spirit to the person. Hopefully, they will see the issues and draw the conclusion on their own.

For instance, if someone is spreading lies about you as pastor, you will need to confront the specific lie and discover why they have lied. More than likely, this person has grown up with poor role models. They have seen authority figures misuse their power. In a sense, this approach will require that the pastor help straighten out some of an individual's skewed thinking. A pastor may want to encourage the individual to identify and sort through unrealistic expectations and begin to reparent themselves.

FEAR HINDERS REPENTANCE

To encourage an individual to genuinely repent, a pastor will need to seek God's wisdom. He or she will also have to deal with the individual's fears.

Before a person lets you pray for them, they will need assurance that whatever made him or her vulnerable to operating with a Jezebel spirit will be eliminated. The door of access to this spirit of fear must be discovered, closed, sealed, and covered.

An individual must also feel safe around a pastor and others who are ministering to him or her. Love and wisdom must be clearly demonstrated in order for ministry to Jezebel to succeed. Simply having good intentions will not reassure the individual.

A myriad of fears may drive the individual. It may be a fear of those in authority or a fear of those who are perceived as a threat. Discovering the root problem or access point that allowed this spirit to infiltrate will greatly facilitate the healing process. This will also help the person to refuse the same spirit in future situations. For example, if a Jezebel spirit entered through a time when the person was feeling rejected, the specific situation that occurred should be identified. Therefore, the next time the individual is rejected—or perceives rejection—he or she will not resort to the old behavior of control and manipulation.

When you attempt to deliver someone with the Jezebel spirit, they will be afraid of losing everything. What you see as a demonic spirit, they will see as their protector. They have mistakenly believed they are operating in the Holy Spirit. Therefore, they will believe that all their perceptions, opinions, words of knowledge, and dreams have come from God. The pastor's task is to dismantle this lie so that the individual can recognize the deception in which they have walked.

Normally, the person will need to be assured that God is at work to help him or her effectively resist and overcome a Jezebel spirit. Over time, this process of discernment and not yielding to old habits will build godly character. Remember: God is faithful to complete the healing that He has begun in the individual's life (Philippians 1:6).

REMORSE FOR GETTING CAUGHT

Remorse has underlying tones of regret for being caught. In addition, it suggests the possibility that they will do it again at another time. It takes a seasoned leader to discern the difference between repentance and remorse.

Church discipline must continue until true repentance comes forth, evidenced by godly sorrow (2 Corinthians 7:10). Godly sorrow is a sign of a broken will. Even if the individual repents, they must not remain or be placed in *any* form of leadership. The individual's soul and spirit must first be renewed and restored. All of this takes time to heal properly. We must understand that this process involves more than forgiveness. It involves inner healing, which usually takes several years. Therefore, if the individual wants to start leading a small group, do not bow to their pressure. Rushing to reinstate the person in leadership-would be like sending a former alcoholic into a bar to witness. Wisdom cautions us not to do it.

THE PROBLEM OF DENIAL

Problems arise if the person denies having issues of control or manipulation. Surprisingly, denial often happens after a private meeting occurs where the person admitted to having the problem.

When these problems resurface, they will have a greater sting. Since you have already played your hand, Jezebel will begin to anticipate what you will say and craft a clever rebuttal. Piece by piece, they will dismantle your entire case against them.

A pastor, who should have already informed the leadership of Jezebel, will need to gather the leadership team around him or her. Together, they will need to address and confront the individual quickly. You do not want this problem to linger, because it will brew to hurricane strength. Furthermore, repentance must be required immediately. I recommend following the twelve steps outlined for pastors in Chapter 10.

Since God requires two witnesses, you must have witnesses when you confront an individual with a Jezebel spirit. Witnesses may be necessary if the individual later lies or twists what was said. By having witnesses present, you ensure that proper and necessary action will be taken.

In addition, witnesses provide a power of agreement to bind and to loose. Together, you can bind the Jezebel spirit and its power from affecting future events in your church.

REMOVAL

If the individual is unrepentant and unwilling to undergo deliverance, they must be removed from the church. Scripture describes a man who challenged pastoral authority and who was severely corrected and removed from fellowship (1 Corinthians 5:4-5). These severe corrections require that leaders continue to demonstrate love, character, and valor.

RESTORATION

Because the apostle Paul was interested in the Kingdom and not in harboring a personal vendetta, several years later he noticed the Corinthian man's godly sorrow who had been removed from the church (2 Corinthians 2:4-11). However, the church leadership had failed to notice it. So, Paul encouraged them to take the man back into fellowship.

Likewise, after the individual has been removed, if the stronghold over the person is truly broken, then we must forgive and restore the person to the church. Obviously, restoration must be done wisely by those who can accurately judge the individual's sincerity and depth of repentance.

JEZEBEL'S DESTRUCTION

Jehu, ruler of the longest-lived dynasty in Israel, was anointed by Elisha and given a mandate by God to eliminate Jezebel and the house of Ahab (2 Kings 9:7).

Jehu wasted no time in carrying out his mandate. At his command, Jezebel's servants threw her down from her lofty perch on the wall. Interestingly, her servants were eunuchs who did not yield to her seductions. They were able to carry out Jehu's orders, so that true watchmen of God could stand there (2 Kings 9:33).

Likewise, anyone who is going to confront Jezebel must become a spiritual eunuch. They must not be tempted by the lust of the flesh, the lust of the eyes, or the pride of life (1 John 2:16). Such a person must be as resolute and uncompromising as Jehu and as incapable of being seduced as Jezebel's eunuchs.

In this hour, I pray that godly pastors of kingly character, valor, and strength will arise. I pray that with courage, they will lay an axe at the root of this demonic spirit that seeks to destroy prophets, emasculate pastors, and pervert the Body of Christ. As God's people, we need to love what He loves and hate what He hates. We do not need to shrink back and become afraid of addressing and correcting lawlessness and rebellion that defiles the Body of Christ.

THE ANTIDOTE

Since lawlessness is a disease of our culture today, pastors will need to take a proactive approach. I recommend having on-going teaching in a church on the topic of spiritual authority and lawlessness.

Chapter 12

RECLAIMING FOLLOWERS OF JEZEBEL

THERE WAS NOTHING TO do, but return to what he knew—fishing. For three years Peter had ministered beside Jesus. He had been included in His inner circle of disciples and been on the Mount of Transfiguration. In the end, however, Peter denied his Lord when it counted the most.

Even though Peter was thrilled to see Jesus after the resurrection, he felt a sense of shame because of his denial. Jesus knew that Peter had repented. Yet Peter needed encouragement to embrace his calling. As they finished eating breakfast by the seashore, Jesus asked Peter a series of questions designed to mend his broken spirit and restore him to the Lord (John 21:15-17).

In a similar way, individuals who are being freed from a Jezebel spirit will also need to be restored. They will need to be reminded that if we are faithful to confess our sins, the Lord is faithful to forgive us our sins and cleanse us from the effects of unrighteousness (1 John 1:9). What sin could be worse than Peter's denials of Jesus at the most crucial moment in Jesus' life? Although He felt the sting of the betrayal from one of his closest friends, Jesus forgave Peter.

No wounds are more painful in life than those we suffer at the hands of our friends, especially those whom we follow. These wounds will need to be touched by the Lord so that He can bring healing and wholeness. It makes no difference whether you are a pastor or a church member. All wounds from a Jezebel spirit must be healed.

Jesus anointed His Church to carry on the work of His Kingdom—healing the brokenhearted and setting free those who have been held captive by the wicked one (Isaiah 61:1). True healing comes when the following areas are addressed:

TEARING DOWN STRONGHOLDS

Ministry to Jezebel's followers will involve tearing down mental strongholds. In his book, *Healing the Nations*, John Sandford defines a mental stronghold as a practiced way of thinking that has become ingrained and automatic. It has a life and a will of its own. Strongholds are areas of the mind where we are held captive and our perceptions are completely distorted.

For example, I once had a silly discussion with my wife over the color of flowers along the roadside. I saw them as coral flowers. My wife saw them as white flowers. I "knew" I was right, because of my perceptions. I could not understand why she kept insisting the flowers were white. It wasn't until I removed my yellow-tinted sunglasses that I realized my wife was right! The flowers were actually white. The tinted lens had distorted the flowers' color and caused them to appear coral. Because I thought I was right, I responded indignantly to my wife's protests with passionate conviction. Yet, something had distorted how I viewed the situation. This illustrates how strongholds can distort our perception of an actual situation. We can interpret what happens, through lenses that are tainted and distorted by our wounds.

As you walk out your healing, you will need to bravely take a ruthless, personal assessment. It may be a shock to face reality and abandon your delusions. To open the door to self-discovery and self-disclosure, we will need God's grace. As we open our hearts to the truth about ourselves, the healing journey begins.

The following areas may have allowed the enemy easy access to our lives and fueled the drive to follow someone with a Jezebel spirit.

1. AN EMOTIONAL DEPENDENCY TOWARD OTHERS

People who follow someone with a Jezebel spirit tend to be emotionally dependent. They have a great inner drive to be connected with someone or to have a special relationship with a particular person to heal their wounded self-esteem. While it is normal to need other people, overdependent people feel as if they need someone in their life all the time, fearing physical or emotional abandonment. Instead of developing healthy intimacy, they seek to enmesh and merge with another. Trying to fill the loneliness, emptiness, and lack of self-love has driven them into codependent and often abusive relationships.

God has placed deep within every human spirit a heart cry. He designed us to be relational people with a longing for fellowship. But unless we allow our heavenly Father to fill that core need, our identity will become like that of an orphan. We will drift along, desperately looking to others to meet our needs and adopt us.

For such wounded souls, God is the healing balm. God gently woos and draws us to the only place where our deep hunger can be satisfied. Our misplaced longings can *only* find true rest in God the Father. Then as the Holy Spirit bears witness that God is our Father, He will also attest that we are His children (Romans 8:16). We will be given a spirit of adoption, by which we are enabled to cry "Abba, Daddy!" To know Him as Father is to love and accept His authority over us. Our dependency then falls on Him, rather than on another person.

2. AN ATTITUDE OF FEARFULNESS

Fear usually begins through unholy imagination. The mental aspect of our soul begins to focus on things that can potentially harm us. A spirit of fear then takes root in our soul.

Often those who follow someone with a Jezebel spirit will have a history of enslaving fears of neglect, of rejection, of being punished, of loneliness, and perhap of missing the will of God. These fears arise from our past experiences and are applied to today's circumstances.

A spirit of fear is a sign of spiritual enslavement. It leads someone into being subservient to the control of others. For those who followed Jezebel, they will have a recurring fear of being deceived again.They will be tempted to view authority as being tyrannical. All fears of being dominated or controlled must be brought to the Cross. Recent fears, as well as those rooted in childhood, must be reckoned as dead on the Cross (Romans 6:11) in order for new life to begin (2 Corinthians 5:17). Dying to these fears will free us to relate to others without fear.

To begin our healing, we must ask God to show us the circumstances that led to opening our soul to fear. We must—through faith—cast down what the Bible calls "vain imaginations." By faith, we need to cleanse ourselves of fear and ask another Christian who is free from fear to stand with us in agreement. We also need to ask God to fill us with love, power, and sound reasoning because His perfect love casts out our fear.

When our mind is ruled by our spirit, we will focus on the virtues that spring forth from the Lord. We will be able to concentrate on that which is true, noble, just, pure, lovely, of a good report, virtuous and praiseworthy (Philippians 4:8).

3. A FEAR OF DECISION MAKING

When we relinquish our choices and decisions to another person, we will run the risk of causing our spirit to atrophy. It will lose the ability to discern what is from God. We also risk falling into the sin of lawlessness (Hebrews 5:14).

God gives us our ability to exercise free will—the freedom to make choices and decisions. Without a will, we would be like Data, the android on Star Trek that only did whatever he was told. By giving us free will, God empowers us to follow through and complete decisions we have made. Therefore, when we yield our will to another person, we have given them the right to make decisions on our behalf. We then forfeit our ability to receive insight and revelation directly from God. In doing so, we have made Jezebel our idol, who now takes the place of God.

When we avoid making decisions, our motive may lie rooted in self-condemnation and a sense of incompetence. We may have never been taught how to make responsible decisions. Or, we may feel incapable of making a good decision. If that's the case, we may have been raised in a harsh and critical home where the punishment for making a mistake outweighed the actual offense. We could never do anything good enough!

Therefore, we avoid making a decision due to the fear of being penalized for making a bad one. To compensate, we will acquire a mind-set that anticipates failure. We will be afraid to take risks. Instead, we listen to the whispers in our head that predict eventual failure. Shying away from responsibility, we then grow up unable, indifferent, unmotivated, or disinterested in making decisions.

To overcome a fear of failure, we will need to change how we think. We will need to learn how to envision success, *not* failure. The healthier we become, the more we will be able to practice making good decisions. Remember, God is faithful to show His will to any who humbly seek it and are willing to obey it.

4. A DEEP SENSE OF SHAME

Shame is the sense of feeling fundamentally bad, inadequate, defective, unworthy, or not measuring up to some standard. Many will need healing from a deep sense of shame.

At some point in our life, all of us feel shame. But for an individual who has followed Jezebel, shame will be a constant painful memory. They will doubt their ability to hear from God, as if they are eternally flawed or blemished. They may believe that God is disgusted with them. Therefore, it may be helpful to remind them that all is *not* lost. Instead, a great lesson was learned.

It's often at our lowest point that we discover the wonder of God's amazing and profound grace. Grace is contrary to shame. While shame brings depression, grace brings hope and lightheartedness.

Grace refers to God's undeserved kindness directed toward us. It is unearned and unrepayable. Through God's grace, we are able to bond with our loving heavenly Father who longs to lavish His great love upon us. As we embrace His Son Jesus, the atoning sacrifice for our sins, He calls us His "sons and daughters." When we journey through the "dark night of the soul," we may be able to hear God whisper to us, "I love and accept you. The plans I have for you are for good and not for evil" (Jeremiah 29:11).

5. *A FEAR OF TRUSTING AGAIN*

Whenever we appeal to another person for our spiritual strength, our heart turns away from the Lord. We have allowed the other person to be our source of strength.

Scripture admonishes us to place our trust in the Lord (Psalm 37:3; Psalm 71:5; Proverbs 3:5; Isaiah 50:10). Personally, I do this by quieting my heart and looking to God. Knowing that I belong to Him helps me to trust and obey His will for my life. Knowing what He wants me to do, moment by moment, is a daily quest. God calls us to live out our faith by trusting in Him. Prayer helps me to wait on God for His direction instead of acting impulsively in my own self-interests. When we put our trust in God, He enables us to trust the spiritual authority that He has placed in our lives (1 Peter 2:13-3:6; 5:5-6).

164

Bonding with God is the basis for rebuilding relationships with others. The stronger our bond with God, the greater our ability to form healthy relationships with others. Our courage to trust again flows from our connectedness with God.

While Jesus touched many people, He only disclosed His heart to a few close friends who were committed to Him. Likewise, we should only trust another individual to the degree that we see Jesus, and not a religious pretense, manifested in their life (Micah 7:5-13).

6. THE CONSEQUENCES OF NAIVETÉ

Naiveté can place a person at great risk. Naiveté implies that an individual is simple-minded, ignorant, foolish, and able to be ensnared and mislead (Proverbs 27:12). As such, they are gullible and are often exploited by Jezebel. Those who are controlling and manipulative will instinctively sniff out an opportunity to take advantage of them.

Naiveté can also foster our need to idolize another individual. Whenever we feel an excessive admiration toward someone, we will begin to form unrealistic expectations of them. We will exaggerate their good points and become blinded to their faults. This unhealthy esteem and affection actually hinders, rather than edifies, the person.

Throughout Scripture, we are encouraged to embrace wisdom, knowledge, and discretion which preserves our life and protects us from evil (Proverbs 2:10-13). Being wise and discrete will repel those who seek to oppress and to dominate us.

It is never too late to learn godly wisdom, discretion, and discernment. No matter how many mistakes may lie in your past, God's mercies are new every morning

(Lamentations 3:22-23). His ability to forgive is greater than your ability to fail.

7. *A LOSS OF JOY AND INNOCENCE*

A loss of joy will be evident in the life of someone who is recovering from the pain of following Jezebel. Their withered souls will make it difficult for them to express their emotions. They will begin to slide into a dark depression. When they begin to embrace God's grace, their joy will return, bringing strength.

God has created us to be *full* of joy. Knowing Him intimately brings joy, which enriches our life. I have discovered that joy is like a fountain of youth. It prevents, alleviates, cures the diseases of our soul (Proverbs 17:22), and gives us spiritual vitality. Experiencing joy also empowers us to cultivate healthy relationships with others (Nehemiah 8:10).

Walking in a deep, abiding sense of joy requires a childlike innocence. Innocence allows us to embrace a simple faith that looks to a loving, heavenly Father to solve all of our dilemmas. With time, as our relationship with the Lord deepens, our spontaneity and childlike innocence will be restored. As we let go of trying to control others, we will stop trying to predict what others will do, and thereby, rediscover a childlike wonder and innocence.

8. *FEARING THE SUPERNATURAL*

Those who have been wounded by Jezebel may fear anything that hints of the supernatural or of the spiritual realm. This fear will come as an overreaction to having been initially deceived. Thus, a thick wall of protection is erected in their soul to guard against further deception.

Sadly, this overreaction will hinder them from appreciating the endless variety of God's supernatural gifts such as dreams and visions. They may regard anything beyond their five senses as being suspicious. They may feel uncomfortable during a worship service when God's presence is powerfully manifested. However, this reaction will only cause them to hold God at arms' length.

Did you realize that supernatural gifts are actually tools by which we attack the enemy's camp? By distaining such gifts, we inadvertantly play into the enemy's plans. We revert back to the old adage, "What we don't know can't harm us."

Our ability to embrace supernatural gifts is founded on knowing God as our loving heavenly Father. As a Father, God yearns to give good gifts to His children. In manifesting His presence supernaturally, we see God's awesome glory and majestic splendor. He is truly a God like no other! For we have come to Mount Zion and to the city of the living God, to an innumerable company of angels (Hebrews 12:22-24).

9. BELIEVING A LIE

Unfortunately, many followers of Jezebel have been deceived by demons, and thereby, blinded to the demonic grip that ensnares them. They have formerly viewed others —even pastors—outside their control as being deceived and demonically influenced.

Jezebel will have portrayed itself as being an elite spiritual force, immune to demonic attack. Those entangled by Jezebel's web of deception will erroneously look to Jezebel, instead of the Lord, as a fortress of protection against the demonic.

Trusting in evil spirits—whether you know them to be evil spirits or not—places you under their authority and false protection. Thus, you have given these spirits keys to your life. Since they provide a harmful authority, you will need deliverance from their domain. If you have an aversion to deliverance, ask God to remove any stronghold that you may have and that blinds you to seeing the answer to your healing.

10. TELLING OTHER VOICES TO STOP

For a season, demonic spirits will test former followers to see if they really mean business. They will need to command the voices and masters in their mind to cease instructing or beguiling them. If these seductive spirits return to tempt him or her, they need to resist them.

From now on, they are free to follow no other voice, but the voice of Jesus. They need to embrace the words of Jesus, "My sheep hear My voice...I know them, and they follow Me" (John 10:27).

11. REFUSING JEZEBEL'S INFLUENCE

Do not receive the counsel, prayers or the laying on of hands from anyone whom you sense has a Jezebel spirit operating in their life. It may be wise to consider getting rid of any personal items—clothing, jewelry, books, music, art, knick-knacks or photos—that have been given to you by Jezebel. These items can represent soul ties that will hinder your journey to freedom. Ask the Lord to show you if you need to destroy such items (Acts 19:19).

12. RECONCILING WITH FAMILY AND FRIENDS

> Therefore if you bring your gift to the altar,
> and there remember that your brother has
> something against you, leave your gift there
> before the altar, and go your way. First be
> reconciled to your brother, and then come and
> offer your gift—Matthew 5:23-24.

While operating under the stronghold of a Jezebel spirit, it is easy to become blinded to the wounds you inflicted on others. Ask the Lord to help you recognize your own actions and to view them through the other person's eyes. This will open your eyes as to how your manipulation and control brought injury to them.

Forgiveness is not the same as excusing someone's behavior. Forgiveness acknowledges the offense and then chooses to not hold that offense against the person. When Jesus Christ died on the Cross, His blood was the payment for our sins so that we could be truly forgiven. Likewise by extending forgiveness to someone, we mirror the depth of God's forgiveness to us.

> Let all bitterness, wrath, anger, clamor, and
> evil speaking be put away from you, with all
> malice. And be kind to one another, tender-
> hearted, forgiving one another, even as God
> in Christ forgave you—Ephesians 4:31-32.

You will need to ask forgiveness of individuals that you have wronged or hurt, and leaders whose church or ministry you have maligned. Ask God to help you in making your confession. Communicate that you realize your actions were intolerable. As you feel some of their pain, you will be able to ask sorrowfully for their forgiveness.

You may feel compelled to make amends with your loved ones. Such reconciliation will bring about restoration and greater spiritual release. As a result, curses spoken by the spirit of Jezebel are rendered void and powerless.

The process of forgiveness will take time. You will need time to recuperate and reenter old routines. Family chores that have been left undone will need to be resumed, not begrudgingly but in an attitude of gratefulness. This kindness will help restore healthy relationships. Godly counselors can also be beneficial in the healing process.

13. CREATING HEALTHY RELATIONSHIPS

The energy needed to initiate new relationships may be hampered by lethargy, which comes as a by-product of being dominated by another person. Walking through the process of healing will be tiring. You may feel exhausted both physically and emotionally. At the same time, you will need to be encouraged to participate in church activities. You may need to be encouraged not to isolate from others. You will need to be motivated to embrace self-discipline and to establish healthy boundaries with others. In this way, you will recapture a spirit-led will.

14. LEARN HUMILITY

Humility and obedience always lead us to God. They open a door for God's grace to be extended to us. True repentance is the ultimate act of humility. We know that "God resists the proud, but gives grace to the humble" (James 4:6). Each day, we need to ask the Holy Spirit to convict us, so that any hurtful or harmful thing in our life is exposed. Then, we should come to our heavenly Father and to one another with godly sorrow. True repentance will always set us free from bondage.

15. TRUST JESUS DAILY

When our needs for love go unmet, it will breed codependency and the impulse to "bend into" another person. Instead of looking to another person who is limited and unreliable, we need to develop our spiritual well-being. Each day, we need to look to Jesus, who is sufficient to supply all our needs—emotional, physical, spiritual, and relational. He is the all-sufficient One and in Him resides the fullness of life (John 1:4).

> Trust in the Lord with all your heart, and lean not on your own understanding; in all your ways acknowledge Him, and He shall direct your paths—Proverbs 3:5-6.

16. CLEANSING PRAYER

A follower of Jezebel may want to pray these words of repentance and deliverance along their journey toward wholeness: "Heavenly Father, I need Your Holy Spirit to help me *not* think and live according to my old ways. I place my childhood fears and bloodline curses behind me. I ask You to cancel them, by faith in the Name of Jesus. I choose not to be enslaved to them any longer.

"I lay aside my fear of facing the pain from past friendships, romances, lovers, and relatives. I renounce all pride, bitterness, occult, and Satanic spirits. I renounce the spirits of lying and self-exaltation. I choose to hate rebellion and witchcraft. I will *not* walk in these any longer. Instead, I want to respond in godliness when I am tested by these deceiving spirits. I ask You to remove any mental strongholds and to help me think and see clearly.

"I choose to *not* listen to other spiritual voices. I choose to listen to Your Voice. From this time forth, I will *not* trust in lying spirits nor the spirits who claim to offer me protection from evil. I close every door to Satan. I will *not* seek a false defense to shield myself from wrong, exploitation or harm. Instead, I look to You and place my trust in You to protect me from the harm of well-meaning people and from demonic spirits. I choose You, Holy Spirit, to be my defender. I choose You, Jesus, to be my Savior.

"Lord Jesus Christ, please forgive my sins. I confess I have *not* loved rightly. Instead, I have resented others. I recognize this as sin. I confess this to you now and I choose to forgive those who have hurt me. By Your blood, I forgive myself as You have forgiven me. I am sorry for my sins. I confess and renounce them, known and unknown. I believe you died on the Cross for my sins, and that you rose from the dead and ascended to God the Father. You now sit at His right hand. With repentance in my heart, I ask You, Lord, to deliver me and to set me free. I ask You to deliver me from the snare of the fowler and to cover me as a shield. Your truth is a shield to me. Under Your wings, I seek refuge.

"I claim Your promise in Scripture: Because I have set my love upon You, You will deliver me. You will set me on high because I have known Your Name. I will call upon You, and You will answer me. You will be with me in trouble. You will deliver me and honor me" (Translation of Psalm 91:14-15).

In Summary

It is my prayer that those who have been cleansed and healed of the Jezebel spirit and its influence will become strong in the Lord Jesus and go forth to build the Kingdom of God. May the Lord's wisdom greatly increase in His Church, and may He grant us the ability to minister restoration to one another.

As the Holy Spirit is being poured out upon the Lord's menservants and maidservants in these last days (Acts 2:18), may God-breathed prophesy, signs and wonders arise and transform our generation. May His Kingdom come, may His will be done on Earth as it is in Heaven!

Appendix A

14 CHARACTERISTICS OF THE JEZEBEL SPIRIT

HERE ARE SOME OF the characteristics that accompany the work of this demonic spirit. Please keep in mind that a person heavily influenced by a Jezebel spirit may do many of the following, at one time or another, although not necessarily in the order described.

A single characteristic does not indicate that someone has a "full blown" Jezebel spirit. It may simply mean that the person is still spiritually and emotionally immature. However, whenever a combination of several of the fourteen characteristics exists, there is a strong indication that an individual is influenced by a Jezebel spirit. Also, remember that one characteristic may be clearly noticeable, but other traits may be hidden and yet, profound. A prolonged manifestation of any of these traits warrants a closer look at the individual and the situation.

1. While it's almost unrecognizable at first, this individual is threatened by a prophet, who is the main target of concern. Although the person will seem to have prophetic gifts, their aim is to actually control those who move in the prophetic realm.

2. To increase their favor, this individual often zeroes in on a pastor and church staff, and then seeks to find the weakest link in order to subdue it. Their eventual goal is to run the church.

3. Seeking to gain a popular and pastoral endorsement, this individual will form strategic affiliations with people who are perceived by others to be spiritual or influencial.

4. To appear spiritual, this individual will seek recognition by manipulating things to gain an advantage. Such individuals often conjure up dreams and visions from their imaginations, or they borrow them from others.

5. When this individual receives initial recognition, they usually respond with false humility. However, this trait is short-lived.

6. When confronted, this individual will become defensive. They will justify their actions with phrases like, "I'm just following God" or "God told me to do this."

7. This individual will often alledge having great spiritual insight into church government and affairs, but he or she will not appeal to proper authority. They will *first* appeal to others. The person's opinion often becomes the "last word" on matters, thereby elevating their thoughts above the pastor's. But if their revelation is from God, this person will usually prefer to share it instead of praying it.

8. With impure motives, this individual will seek out others. They seem to desire to have "disciples" and need constant affirmation from their followers.

9. Without any accountability, this individual prefers to pray for people in isolated situations—in a corner or in another room. Thus, innuendoes and false "prophetic" words cannot be easily challenged.

10. Eager to gain control, this person will gather others and seek to teach them. While the teachings may begin correctly, "doctrine" is established that is not supported by the Word of God.

11. Deceiving others by soulish prophecy or by giving words that someone wants to hear, this individual seeks to gain credibility. They prophesy half-truths or little known facts, as if they were from God. Such individuals may also take advantage of someone else's poor memory by twisting their previous prophecies to make it seem as if their words had come to pass.

12. Although the laying on of hands is biblical, this individual likes to impart a "higher" level in the spirit—or break down walls that have held someone back—by laying on of their hands. Yet, this person's touch is actually a curse. Instead of a holy blessing, an evil spirit may be imparted.

13. Masking poor self-esteem with spiritual pride, this individual wants to be seen as the most spiritual person in the church. They may be the first to cry, wail, or mourn—claiming a burden from God. However, they are no different from the Pharisees who announced their gifts to be seen by men.

14. Sadly, this individual's family life is shakey. The individual may be single or married. If married, their spouse is usually weak spiritually, unsaved, or miserable. This person begins to dominate and control everyone in their family.

FUNDAMENTALS OF STRONGHOLDS

STRONGHOLDS ARE AREAS of the mind where darkness reigns. It is a system of logic, rooted in a lie, that we have come to accept. It is a system of thought that forms behind any habitual response, addiction, fixation, compulsion, obsession, and/or inordinate fear. Strong holds are any thought pattern alien to the Word of God. As such, they are a mental or emotional "command post" to which the enemy has access. This mental or emotional word system is designed to create misinformation and thereby affect our decision-making ability. Consequently, strongholds will keep us from embracing Christlikeness.

Here are some fundamental truths about how strongholds operate and hold people captive:

1. Strongholds form the primary strategy of Satan's work around the world and in our lives.

2. Strongholds form presuppositions that distort our perceptions of everything we encounter.

3. Everyone has strongholds in their lives.
4. None of us are as free as Jesus' death on the Cross was purposed to make us. Remember, the blood of Jesus cleanses us from all sin (1 John 1:7). His blood is a weapon that disables strongholds.
5. As my friend, Jack Taylor says, "If you are as free as you want to be, then you are as free as you're going to be—until your desire changes."

STRONGHOLDS IN OPERATION

1. Strongholds prevent or retard our emotional and spiritual growth and maturity.
2. Strongholds cause conflict, separation, and divorce in marriage. In the church, strongholds cause division. They provoke bitterness, jealousy, anxiety, and depression.
3. Strongholds empower Satan and his demons, while grieving the angels and the Holy Spirit.
4. Strongholds keep individuals from their personal destiny and keep them from accepting what Christ has made them to be.
5. Strongholds are a foothold or a place that the devil has in us (Ephesians 4:22).
6. Strongholds produce financial disorder and will bring about spiritual disorientation.
7. Strongholds weaken our body and make us vulnerable to diseases.
8. Strongholds provoke us to respond to others in ways that even we don't understand. They fragment attempted friendships and steal our joy and hope.
9. Strongholds stifle our faith and distort Scripture. They cloud and darken our minds and imprison our spirit.

10. Strongholds can only be killed at the root. They cannot be removed simply by addressing the manifestation.
11. Strongholds allow us to give a begrudging love, at best. They keep us from forgiving others.

MY PRAYER

Here's a prayer that I offer every day for my family and myself. Feel free to adapt it to your daily devotion with the Lord:

Lord, I humbly admit that I have mental strongholds in my life that distort my perception of what You are doing. I ask You to tear these down so that I can perceive clearly.

Today, I loose myself to the Holy Spirit and to walk in the fullness of Your purpose for my life. I know that I am capable of doing much more in You than I allow to happen. Therefore, I loose my spirit, soul, and body to be *totally* yours today! Amen.

APPENDIX C

AMY'S STORY

T HE FOLLOWING STORY IS a true account of a woman who followed someone with a Jezebel spirit. It is my prayer that her testimony will be an encouragment to those who have succumbed to this spirit. I pray that her story will be prayerfully considered. May Amy's testimony shine the way to true freedom for those who are called to bear the testimony of Jesus, which is the spirit of prophecy.

AMY'S STORY

My first encounter with a Jezebel spirit began several years ago. I had gone forward for prayer following a worship service at church. I desperately needed physical and emotional healing. For several years, I had been to many specialists and psychiatrists, but they never seemed to help. I was exhausted and at the end of my rope. After prayer, a woman near the front of the church approached me. She seemed eager to help and sounded very spiritual. She asked for my telephone number and expressed an interest in calling me. Although I had no idea why, I gave her my phone number.

When the woman called, I told her about an inner voice that seemed clear, distinct, and almost audible. It would teach me something in the Bible and told me about my condition and how to become free. She said that she, too, had heard its voice. She seemed like a godly woman, an intercessor, and seemed to know a great deal about the Bible. Then, I began to trust her.

THE TEACHING

We started studying the Bible and pursuing revelation together. She insisted that I could deliver myself through Scripture. She emphasized deliverance. She was always "pro-God," but very subtly, Jesus was never mentioned. She said that we—not Jesus—were the mediators between God and man. We began using the names of God to deliver ourselves. Thereby, we were learning a newfound freedom in the spirit. Although I desperately wanted to escape my emotional pain, I spent four years delivering myself from one thing after another—or in her lingo: "taking back the land."

Looking good to this woman became very important to me. Later, I realized that she fed off my spirit and my adulation of her. She began to stress spiritual disciplines such as fasting. I would fast to receive her approval, as well as God's. At first, the two of us seemed to be on a journey together. If I learned something, I would tell her and she would respond. If she learned something, she would tell me and I would do it. Then, we compiled our thoughts into a teaching on deliverance. If someone had problems with a particular spirit, we would offer to minister to them.

AMY'S MARRIAGE DETERIORATED

As our relationship developed, my relationship with my husband deteriorated. In fact, he planned to leave me. I thought that he—not I—was the problem. I was blind to any other perspective. This woman only made my marriage problems worse. Whenever she came to my home, she showed little respect for my husband's feelings. If he came home while we were visiting, she would overstay her visit and tie up my time. My husband, who worked two jobs, wanted time to relax and be with his family. Yet, my friend was thoughtless, rude, and insensitive to my husband and my family.

A GUISE OF SUBMISSION

I thought I was submissive to my husband because I was compliant with certain things. But to be honest, I was not a submissive wife. I was still calling the shots and getting my way. If I didn't get my way, I would continually voice my displeasure. Tension continued to mount in my marriage. Although it's easy to talk about submission, it's difficult to live it out daily.

CLOTHING GIVEN, DREAMS RECEIVED

When a new pastor joined our church, he spoke on the Jezebel spirit. Presumptively, my friend and I decided that he was a false prophet. I even had a dream that he had a Jezebel spirit! So, I decided to counsel him about getting some deliverance. I worked up some notes and gave them to this pastor. He politely took them without saying much. After that, my friend and I thought he was okay. We even took pride that he "received" my teaching. However, he knew how to detect a Jezebel spirit and he was quickly clued into both of us.

CONVICTION

Four years later someone exposed my prideful deception. My husband had become a Christian during that time. One evening, my sister and her husband, along with another couple, prayed for me and my husband. I could tell my sister was hesitant. But as soon as she began to speak, I began to weep.

She said I had a spirit of deception and that my friend had a Jezebel spirit. At first, I heard a roar in my ears. "This can't be true," I thought. Horrified, I kept quiet. But then, another quieter voice that seemed to come from my heart like a whisper said, "Receive this, it is true." As I did, the other voice left.

When I got home, I threw all my notes and teachings into the garbage. Then, I went to my closet and pulled out clothes that she had given me. I separated myself from this woman for months. During that time, I was hurting and still questioned if the revelation was true. Some days, I was tempted to deny what my sister had said. I thought I had understood the Jezebel spirit and had even delivered myself of that spirit. Even though I had done much to distance myself from this spirit, it seemed as if it was still inside my mind and my body.

PARTING

In retrospect, I think I was fearful. My thoughts were full of anxiety and insecurity. I thought that I needed this woman to lean on—not realizing that the Lord had given my husband to me to serve that purpose. All along, the Lord warned me of this woman, but I had not broken off the relationship. I cannot blame my friend for what was inside of me. I cannot blame her for the voice I heard. Looking back, I realized that I had heard this voice before I ever met her. But the voice and the thoughts inside of me became more prominent when I joined forces with her.

Separating from this woman was like losing my mother. For years, I had fed off her spirit and vice versa. Sadly, after all those years, I had no real spiritual fruit or supernatural power. Thinking I was wise, I discovered that I had lived a life of deceit and rebellion.

HUNGRY FOR MYSTERIES

I had hungered to know the great mysteries of God. Then, the Lord said to me softly, "You sought to know all knowledge and all mysteries about Me, but the greatest mystery is that while you were yet a sinner, Christ died for you." It was a powerful and humble revelation for me.

A REVEALING DREAM

Shortly thereafter, the Lord gave me a dream. My husband and two sons were on a hay wagon. I started to climb into the wagon, but my husband said, "Who is going to push the wagon?" Filled with anger and resentment, I climbed off the wagon. "I have been working all day long, and now I have to push this wagon home," I complained.

But surprisingly, when I began to push the wagon, it wasn't a hard thing to do. It was really light. Still, I could not understand why my husband wouldn't help me.

When I told the dream to my pastor, I said, "Sometimes with my husband, I feel like I'm talking to a wall!" My pastor graciously encouraged me to pray the passage in Ephesians 5 so that my husband would come into his rightful position.

As soon as I got home, I got on my knees. "God, I've gone through four years of doing what I thought was holy. I thought that I knew how to pray, but I realize that I do not." As I was saying those words, I remembered my dream. Suddenly I saw a vision of myself climbing onto the wagon. My two sons had full rein. I said nothing. I stopped telling everyone what to do and where they should be. Instead, I was riding along on the wagon! I, then, saw my husband get off the wagon.

The Lord spoke to me very clearly, "The wall you've sensed in your husband was not because your husband was unwilling to push, but because you were unwilling to let him push." With great mercy, God showed me that I was the wall in the relationship with my husband. I had not allowed my husband to hear from God for himself. I realized my attitude had been, "God, you tell me, and then I'll tell my husband." I quickly repented for my prideful heart.

ASKING FORGIVENESS

I had one final thing to do. The Lord dealt with me about what I had taught. I was grieved about misleading people. The Lord told me, "You're going to have to ask their forgiveness for what you've shared with others." I had shared the teachings and revelations of Jezebel with others.

The Holy Spirit prompted me to listen to my pastor's teaching tape on the Jezebel spirit. I was deeply convicted by the reference in Revelation to "those who do not hold to this teaching." I realized that I had held onto the teaching of this demonic spirit, and shared it with others. The passage revealed God's judgment for Jezebel and her followers. My spirit was deeply grieved.

At that time, God granted me a deep repentance. I confessed to God, "The voice which I received was not Your voice. The teaching was not Your teaching." That night, I engaged in spiritual warfare. Yet, I confessed to God: "This teaching that I have believed was from Satan." The next morning, the light dawned and my testimony became apparent. I shared it with my pastor.

He told me that a year earlier he had seen me sitting in the woman's car. He sensed that we were involved with this spirit. He wanted to tell me, but the Lord would not allow him. He knew that I would simply react in rebellion. He had godly wisdom to wait until the God-appointed time.

KEYS TO FORGIVENESS AND HUMILITY

It should be easy to forgive someone. Since I have been forgiven much, I need to love much. And yet, I was in such pain. Why was I still holding on to my anger and resentment? The Lord Jesus says cast our burdens and cares upon Him. But I guess that I hadn't really cast them upon Him, until now. I humbled myself before my husband and asked his forgiveness. "I've made so many mistakes in trying to lead our family. But I need to show grace to let you lead us."

In times past, I would not trust my husband's decisions unless I had a part in making them. Today, I am learning to trust my husband just as I trust God. I have chosen to be submissive to him according to Ephesians 5:22, and to love the Lord Jesus Christ and Him only.

The Jezebel spirit has a pretense of exalting God, but it always exalts self. This spirit almost destroyed my marriage as well as my life. I have seen that spirit do the same to other women and their families.

RECOMMENDED READING

Barclay, Mark T. *The Sin of Lawlessness: A Lethal Practice.*
Midland, MI: Mark T. Barclay Publication, 1989.

Berry, Carmen Renee, M.S.W. and Mark W. Baker,
Ph.D. *Who's to Blame?* Colorado Springs:
Pinion Press, 1996.

Carter, Les, Ph.D. and Frank Minirth, M.D. *The
Anger Workbook.* Nashville: Thomas Nelson,
Inc., 1993.

Devenish, David. *Demolishing Strongholds.* Milton Keynes,
England: Word Publishing, 2000.

Gibson, Noel and Phyl. *Deliver Our Children From the Evil
One.* Kent, U.K.: Sovereign World, Ltd., 1992.

— *Evicting Demonic Intruders.* Chichester, U.K.: New
Wine Press, 1993.

Godwin, Rick. *Exposing Witchcraft in the Church.* Orlando:
Creation House, 1997.

Groom, Nancy. *From Bondage to Bonding: Escaping
Codependency, Embracing Biblical Love.*
Colorado Springs: NavPress, 1991.

— *Heart to Heart About Men: Words of
Encouragement for Women of Integrity.* Colorado
Springs: NavPress, 1995.

Joyner, Rick. *Epic Battles of the Last Days*. New Kensington, PA: Whitaker House, 1995.

Ketterman, Grace, M.D. and David Hazard. *When You Can't Say "I Forgive You": Breaking the Bonds of Anger and Hurt*. Colorado Springs: NavPress, 2000.

Malone, Henry. *Shadow Boxing*. Irving, TX: Truth Publishing, 1999.

Mellody, Pia. *Facing Love Addiction: Giving Yourself the Power to Change the Way You Love*. San Francisco: HarperCollins Publishers, 1992.

Moore, John L. *The Limits of Mercy*. Nashville: Thomas Nelson, Inc., 1996.

Myer, Joyce. *Managing Your Emotions Instead of Your Emotions Managing You!* Tulsa, OK: Harrison House, 1997.

Payne, Leanne. *The Broken Image: Restoring Personal Wholeness Through Healing Prayer*. Wheaton: Crossway Books, 1981.

Sandford, John. *Healing the Nations: A Call to Global Intercession*. Grand Rapids: Chosen Books, a division of Baker Book House, 2000.

Sandford, John and Mark. *A Comprehensive Guide to Deliverance and Inner Healing*. Grand Rapids: Fleming H. Revell, a division of Baker Book House Company, 1992.

Sandford, John and R. Loren Sandford. *The Renewal of the Mind*. Tulsa: Victory House Publishers, 1991.

Schaumburg, Harry W., Dr. *False Intimacy: Understanding the Struggle of Sexual Addiction.* Colorado Springs: NavPress, 1997.

Smith, Eddie and Alice. *Intercessors and Pastors: The Emerging Partnership of Watchmen and Gatekeepers.* Houston: SpiriTruth Publishing, 2000.

Whiteman, Tom Ph.D. and Randy Petersen *Victim of Love: How You Can Break the Cycle of Bad Relationships.* Colorado Springs: Pinion Press, 1998.

Needless Casualties of War

by John Paul Jackson

Did you you know there are certain types of prayer Satan would *like* you to pray? Is the enemy wounding you with your own sword? Are you or your church experiencing calamities that prayer does not remedy?

Prayer is a powerful weapon, a two-edged sword, not to be wielded carelessly. Although we have authority as the children of God, how we fight can determine our personal consequences in battle.

In this timely book, John Paul Jackson reveals some startling insights that will uncover spiritual strategies of the enemy. Find out how you can protect yourself fron Satan's onslaught and escape his unforeseen and unperceived attacks.

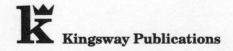 **Kingsway Publications**